ABUSED, OVERUSED AND MEANINGLESS

True stories of Mental Illness of Abusers & the Traumatized, and the Relationship between those Disorders and Opiate Abuse, Accidental Overdose and Suicide

by Kathleen Kush and Chery Jimenez

Dorrance Publishing Co
585 Alpha Drive
Pittsburgh, PA 15238
Visit our website at *www.dorrancebookstore.com*

ISBN: 978-1-4809-9409-6
eISBN: 978-1-4809-8561-2

ACKNOWLEDGEMENTS

Special thanks to National Institute for Mental Health (NIMH) for directing us to publications and studies being done on the topics we are discussing in this book. This includes finding information on PubMed, which sent us to Mayo Clinic publications. We also found great information on the Internet from various sources, including Wikipedia (information confirmed by other sources) and Mental Health America Online.

We especially appreciate all of the survey responses from many therapists and from those who have experienced mental illness themselves or that of loved ones. One-on-one conversations, interviews and life experiences were also tremendous influences, which actually led to the writing of this book.

DEDICATIONS

Chery would like to dedicate this book to her son who lived through his father's dysfunction and yes, through his mother's search, treatments and general craziness, his own issues and yet has become a wonderful young man, despite his childhood. Also, to her brother Jim, who makes her laugh, explains everything to her with patience, makes her feel loved and is the kindest person she knows. To her writing partner Kay, a hero, sister-in-law, best friend, sister, an amazing woman with strength, perseverance and still a pacifist.

She would also like to thank her doctors, Imran Chishti and John Hall and the incredible women who run the D.I.D. website, along with her fellow survivors. Also, her teacher, friend and mentor and his wife, Ernie and Jan Stokes. Because of all of them, she is still here. She would also like to mention some awesome people at Parkside Nursing Home that pulled, pushed and rooted for her.

Peace.

Kathleen would like to dedicate this book to Jim, her loving and patient partner of over 45 years. He has helped her through several life-threatening medical conditions, including depression, during their many years together. Growing up in the same neighborhood and attending the same grade school together, they have been friends all of her life.

To her mother, who instilled the love of reading and honesty, she would like to give her gratitude. To Gloria Steinem, she would like to give her a thumbs-up as being one of her role models.

She would also like to thank her wonderful health providers at the many Grand Strand Regional medical services in Myrtle Beach, SC, who saved her life, as well as her specialists from Charleston. And she especially wants to give a nod to her therapist, Deb, who helped her through rough times and shared the meditation practices of Pema Chodron with her.

Namaste.

DEFINITIONS

*Sources from NIMH, PubMed, Mental Health America Online, Mayo

Narcissist

A mental disorder in which people have an inflated sense of their own importance, a deep need for admiration and a lack of empathy for others. But behind this mask of ultra-confidence lies a fragile self-esteem that's vulnerable to the slightest criticism.

Pathological Liar

A behavior of habitual or compulsive lying. Individuals may be aware they are lying or may believe they are telling the truth. It may manifest over a period of years or a lifetime.

Sometimes pathological liars may be trying to make their own lives seem more exciting.

People affected by this disorder lie for external profit by money, sex and power. Most have above average intelligence.

Psychopath

A person suffering from chronic mental disorder with abnormal or violent social behavior. Most often, they lack the ability to love or establish meaningful relationships. Not all are violent; in fact, some lead relatively normal lives, but will often blame others for their problems.

Sociopath

This is a person with a personality disorder manifesting itself in extreme antisocial attitudes and behavior and lack of conscience. Usually they will blame others for their problems. Bullies.

PTSD

Post Traumatic Stress Disorder is a disorder that develops in some people who have experienced a shocking, scary or dangerous event. It can be temporary or can become chronic. Most experience symptoms with flashbacks, bad and frightening dreams. Symptoms include negative thoughts about self, troubles not remembering features of traumatic events, loss of interest in fun activities and distorted feelings of oneself or the world.

DID: Dissociative Identity Disorder (Multiple Personalities)

This is a condition characterized by the presence of a minimum of two completely different states, where the alter personalities react differently to similar situations. Symptoms include loss of time, being accused of lying or stealing, having apparent strangers recognize them as someone else. They often have other mental disorders such as PTSD. DID is present in about .01% to 1% of adults. Risk factors include severe childhood trauma and sexual abuse.

Bipolar Disorder

This condition is often referred to as manic depression. It is a serious medical condition causing extremes in mood and behavior, although it is not a weakness of family, faith, character or something one can resolve on their own. It can disrupt the lives of those who have it as well as people close to them. People with this condition go from periods of feeling very high, or manic. An episode is the period of depression in between the high periods. There are times of level, or normal moods as well.

When depressed, for approximately two weeks the person will be nervous, with anxiety and worry with feelings of sadness and hopelessness. Bipolar disorder will affect people of all races and backgrounds, and usually starts in the teen years. More than 2.5 million Americans have bipolar disorder. No one knows for sure what causes bipolar disorder, but it is thought to be brain chemistry, family history, stressful or disturbing events and/or use of alcohol and drugs. This often leads to broken relationships, problems with jobs and thoughts of suicide.

Schizophrenia

Schizophrenia is a serious disorder affecting how a person thinks, feels and acts. It is not split or multiple personalities (DID). Most with schizophrenia are non-violent, but may have difficulty expressing normal emotions when around people.

The cause is unclear, but there are theories about genetics, biology of abnormalities in the brain's structure or chemistry. It is not caused by childhood trauma or poor parenting, as is DID. or PTSD. The disorder tends to run in families, and often appears during periods of hormonal, physical or stressful changes; thus, the common occurrence during puberty. It also appears to be triggered by environmental events, and people who are hospitalized for severe infections are at a higher risk, including inside the womb.

Common warning signs of schizophrenia are inappropriate or irrational behavior, a change in personality, irrationally angry or hateful response to loved ones and preoccupation with religion or occult. Some may experience delusions of paranoia or hallucinations of hearing, feeling, seeing or tasting something that doesn't really exist.

Introduction

After spending many long conversations on behavioral patterns and relationships, a few of us became determined to write a story about our lives and those of others who have been traumatized by certain actions. As observers of people, we have become very aware of behavioral traits and when they seem to appear in human relationships. We are not psychiatrists or physicians, but have read extensively on articles by professionals or have taken many classes in the psychiatric studies on the life of living with PTSD, DID, narcissism, sociopathic, schizophrenic and psychopathic problems. We must add that at least one of us is a true believer in nature over nurture, meaning that most behaviors are genetically determined; however, they may be altered by abusive and manipulative action such as bullying or trauma. Also, some of us have conditions such as PTSD, DID and depression with suicidal tendencies, so we've had enough therapy to give us additional, personal insight into this topic.

What sparked our interest to write this book? Not only are we victims of abusive and manipulative people, but we are fortunate enough to find a few kind and gentle individuals who have comforted us during times of distress, even when they weren't sure how to soothe us at the time. We also listened to the news concerning drug/opioid abuse. It seems that no one seems to understand that we need to get to the cause of the abuse. Users will find their drugs or alcohol no matter what. Trying to keep the substances out of the country will not work. They will simply be manufactured synthetically here in the United States. What needs to be done is to analyze and educate our communities on the reasons of abuse. What causes people to become users? Did they grow up in a drug environment? Were they manipulated and abused so much that they dream of escaping reality to find a better place?

Advertisements state that 4 out of 5 heroin addicts started using due to prior use of painkillers. The advertisements lead you to believe that these are drugs that have been prescribed to the users, when the fact is that only a very small percentage received those painkillers legally. Yes, many were prescription drugs, but obtained from family medicine cabinets or purchased illegally. Of course, there are probably a few unscrupulous doctors who overprescribe painkillers to a small amount of the population. However, misleading propaganda will cause those who need pain medicines to make it through the day for genuine illnesses to be restricted to their required dosages of prescriptions due to falsely obtained information.

As our country is suddenly striving to stop opioid addiction, it is time to identify why there is a crisis. Addictions, in most cases, are coping mechanisms to deal with mental illness. The government may succeed with prescription opioids, quite possibly at a cost to those suffering from out-of-control pain due to health issues. They may get "over-prescribing" physicians stopped. The street cost will then rise. But something else will always become available to people who have addictions. We already see the increase of heroin in the United States. It is easily available, low in cost, and spreading from the projects to gated communities.

We should have learned our lesson from the Prohibition years. The temperance societies caused the 18th Amendment to be added to the US Constitution in 1919, prohibiting the sale or use of most alcohol, with very few exceptions. Breweries were forced to engage in different types of businesses with their equipment, ranging from malt extract to ice cream. During this period, bootlegging (illegal production and sale of alcohol) was rampant. Speakeasies, bars that sold illegal alcohol, were everywhere. Although also illegal as of 1909 (some thought this was due to Chinese racism), opium dens were still to be found. The Mafia in Chicago, including Al Capone, profited from bootlegging, and gambling and prostitution reached new heights.

Eventually, citizens blamed Prohibition for the moral decay that was occurring, and the 18th Amendment was repealed in 1933 by the 21st Amendment. In the meantime, many deaths occurred from the use of moonshine which was often manufactured from unusual ingredients, including sawdust.

Why is trying to "fix" the drug problem ineffective? We are presenting to you the crisis behind addictions: mental illness. It has been a subject of shame, ignorance, misdiagnosis and fear. For many years, people hid the fact that people in their families might have a mental illness. It created such a stigma of "something wrong" with the family line, that often the mentally ill person was either hidden away in the home or sent away to an institution or foster family. People with money and connections could send their family members to a sanitarium, hidden from the world by well-paid staff. Other families sent their mentally ill to state-run asylums with atrocious living conditions, inadequate staff, wrong diagnoses and medications and, in some places, regular shock treatments for all of their patients. Still, other people were hidden in the family's attics, basements or a secret room. Those unfortunates were undiagnosed without medication, and many developed even more mental disintegration by their lack of treatment paired with isolation. Don't kid yourselves; this was not only in the 1600s or 1800s or only in third-world countries. It happens every day, and could even be one of your neighbors in the basement.

People of many ages are hidden in nursing homes, left to be forgotten with no correct care or medications. This isolation and being surrounded by people screaming things like "fuck you, God," while hitting themselves over and over does not remedy misdiagnosis, if any. Women might be screaming "help, help," while others are strapped in chairs, often over-medicated with glassy eyes. All of this going on around them: loud noises, chaos and screaming, adds to depression, PTSD, paranoia, anxiety and more. With staff who either scare or ignore the patients, this is just a different face on warehousing people instead of helping them. America's shame.

We can see from many famous and beloved stars and politicians that mental illness is often easy to hide. At other times the person recognizes that something is wrong, but it often becomes too little, too late. Here is just a small example of recognizable people who have been famous, either in front of our eyes or those who never fade in memory. The diagnoses listed come from biographies, the news media, social media, comments from friends or their own revelations in interviews and autobiographies.

There are so many celebrities that we may be reminded of while reading about the few we are discussing here. Their lives, backgrounds, successes and failures, while struggling with mental health, are captivating. We also received similar information from those of you who were brave enough to answer the random surveys sent out to help us write this book. We know that each person's individual pain is never lessened by stories of public figures. Nevertheless, here are some private versions from some famous people.

Michael Jackson was a genius, in many people's opinions. He was gifted with multiple talents: musical, dance and choreography, imagination, visual presentation and more. Yet, he had this talent and helped it grow despite being mentally and physically abused by his father and siblings. They also bullied him about his weight, the size of this nose, acne, skin color, voice and even shyness. Yet, no one in the family did not depend on Michael's finances, even after they learned of his great debt.

Michael suffered from PTSD from the bullying he encountered from his family. Never feeling as if he was physically attractive, he also carried the burden of sexual trauma from exposure from early childhood to sharing a room with all of his brothers and father and their multiple sexual partners in his pre-teen years. As an adult, sometimes he couldn't let family members into his home, not because of malice or anger, but because of an episode of PTSD.

He developed paranoia, feeling that he and his children were never safe. He felt that without bodyguards he could be, literally, ripped into pieces. He instilled fear into his children not to hurt them, but to save them from his own paranoia.

In many ways, Michael Jackson was a narcissist, only caring about his own pleasure. When celebrities admired him, he was on top of the world. When vast numbers of children loved him, he thought he was invincible. Many of us were witnesses to the final crash of his self-esteem. Michael self-medicated through doctors eager for his money without caring about his life. Even at Michael's request, a doctor who knew Michael could die from the medication he wanted basically murdered Michael and robbed us all of his immense talent.

David Bowie was an incredible and daring musician and entertainer. He was not afraid of anything that made him stand out and be the star he became. He was afraid of his older half-brother and his mother's three sisters. It has been said that they all suffered from schizophrenia. Two of his aunts committed suicide. One was institutionalized, receiving a lobotomy for her "nerves." David's brother shared many of David's talents: artistically, in fashion and musically. He loved jazz. Terry would start projects, then abruptly stop and go back to hiding alone in his room. David always wondered why it was

Terry who was crazy instead of himself, or if one day he would wake up with schizophrenia.

Terry committed suicide by throwing himself under a train on January 16, 1985. Very few people knew he was David Bowie's brother, mostly because his father didn't want him to be stigmatized by being related to a crazy boy, only a half-brother. Witnessing David's vast pace and change of personas (one of which was Ziggy Stardust), one can only wonder if David might have missed being diagnosed with DID, or multiple personalities.

John Lennon grew up with a strict aunt and later spent his time with his much more open-minded mother. Just as he was beginning his career, his mother died by being hit by a car. John went into a depression and anger that fueled his already genius musical talent. He was supposedly jealous of George Harrison because he had a nice family life. Later, after the Beatles broke up, he apologized and admitted that he'd intentionally held George back with his talent. He exhibited the traits of a narcissist, even in the Beatles' earliest days when he gave a live radio interview and declared that he and the Beatles were more popular than Jesus Christ. During his life he suffered from several serious bouts with heroin abuse followed by withdrawals.

George Harrison, even with his "normal" family and happy childhood, was bi-polar. He went from complete joy to a desperate search for help to isolating himself from everyone. John Lennon was quoted saying: "George's state of mind was visible depending on if he was worshipping Jesus, the Dalai Lama or heroin." According to sources, that was a statement of truth.

Cher left home at the age of 16 after quitting school. She was bullied at school for being different and belittled by her teachers. She dreamed of stardom, and her single mother (married eight times; however, left her at an orphanage once for several weeks) did not realize that Cher was suffering from dyslexia. Cher moved in with her friend in Los Angeles, where, at the age of 17, became housekeeper to Sonny

Bono, who helped her with her solo singing career. She was insecure of her talent and even her looks. Her family offered no support. Even Sonny would get angry when she had trouble reading lyrics, but she insisted on his being on stage with her due to her insecurity. She treated her depression with alcohol, drugs (although she currently denies she has ever used drugs) and isolation before being diagnosed as being dyslexic. Her talent and self-worth is still holding, going strong in her 70s. What a difference the correct diagnosis can make!

Karen Carpenter was anorexic. People are not born with poor body images or low self-esteem and self-worth. These things are planted by parents, children, teachers and peers until one sees themself the way others do. Make no mistake, depression leads to anxiety. As a performer, her anxiety would deepen to social anxiety. With, no doubt, more psychological damage that was unaddressed due to the fight with anorexia, Karen lost her first mental health battle, along with her life.

Janis Joplin, another female musical phenomenon, also suffered from low self-esteem from bullying during her teen years. She was close to her sister, but felt like an outcast with her parents because she was not happy in the small Texas town associated with the oil industries. During her life, rumors surfaced that she had suffered sexual abuse from her classmates. She was called a pig. She had frizzy hair and pock marks from acne. Both made her insecure and fearful of bullying. She showed signs of PTSD because of this. She was often terrified of being alone, had flashback-style dreams and needed constant reassurance to get up to the stage and sing. She left home because of the redneck atmosphere, but kept returning and trying different colleges, even trying courses in secretarial studies. She was very confused and self-medicated with heroin and Southern Comfort, often given to her by her fans when in concert. Janis had been clean for about three months or more from heroin until she found herself all alone in a hotel. She couldn't get anyone to visit and was afraid to sleep or leave her room. At the bottom of her purse was a baggie of heroin with the set-up, which she had purchased the prior afternoon. For whatever reasons, her mind malfunctioning, not only did she give herself a dose, but used the entire bag which was later found to be a stronger version of heroin than is usually purchased on the streets. She was found dead by a friend when he couldn't reach her when she did not show up for rehearsal. Another loss of supreme talent. A woman who had never been treated for the psychiatric illness behind the heroin.

The death of Robin Williams was a travesty to many of us. He suffered from depression, bi-polarism and narcissism. Robin had a psychiatrist who treated him with the correct medications, but he became an alcoholic and addicted to cocaine. As he joked, if it was shaped like a drug, he ate it. He went to rehab several times and had been clean for years.

Robin feared every audience. He'd wait for someone to read him his movie reviews because he didn't want to be alone if they were bad. Since many were touched deeply when he hung himself, they questioned their own lives. If he could not make it, how could they? But his choice was his alone and we cannot judge him for suicide. People have a right to be too exhausted to go on and face the same thing every day. After his suicide, his wife, who had dealt with the many years of depression, stated that he had recently been diagnosed with Parkinson's. Since he had not had a depressive episode in some time, she could only imagine that his suicide was to protect his family from seeing the pain he would endure.

Countless movie stars fought their own demons: Elizabeth Taylor, Patty Duke, John Belushi, James Dean, Marilyn Monroe, Connie Francis, John Candy and so many more. People who appeared as if they were fine, who had everything, harbored mental illness and hid behind alcohol, prescription medicine, street drugs or acting out in dangerous ways. James Dean wasn't the only celebrity who may or may not have deliberately driven off the road or into the path of an oncoming vehicle.

Authors are not exempt, either. For example, Sylvia Plath struggled with schizophrenia her entire life, ending it with suicide and leaving three children behind. Truman Capote had a very bizarre childhood.

Although he was an author, his main life was ingratiating himself to New York Society. Later he trashed those same people. He was a narcissist and pathological liar, as well as a sociopath/psychopath. He self-medicated with drugs and alcohol, which isolated him. He died at the age of 59 from liver disease and phlebitis, which were complications of multiple drug intoxications.

Henry David Thoreau somewhat fictionalized his book "Walden." He did not live his entire life alone in the woods feeding off of nature. He actually longed for the finer things of life, and made himself welcome in the homes of Emerson and others who tolerated his "artsy" lifestyle.

Edgar Allan Poe lived as darkly as he wrote. He visualized many of his poems and possibly died in an alcoholic stupor without seeking help. He was found in the middle of the street, and it was proclaimed that he died from cerebral inflammation, which was a common term at the time for those who died of disreputable causes. Not much was known of mental illness in the early 1800s.

Certainly, we've had many major politicians throughout the years who have obviously been mentally ill. Often times it was hidden from the public by others in politics. It is more difficult to hide these issues in the present day due to improved, as well as very prying, communication sources.

Joseph Kennedy, Sr. bought and bullied his children's way into politics. He was given the position of Ambassador to England because he had "dirt" on FDR. Joseph had his own secrets. One of his daughters was slow. She looked "retarded" to him as well and he put her in a fancy sanitarium. To make sure she didn't let anyone know she was a Kennedy, he had the doctors lobotomize her. This is just one of the reasons why his wife, Rose, learned to hate him aside from his womanizing and multi-year affair with Gloria Swanson. It has been noted that Joseph was absolutely narcissistic, a psychopath and sociopath. Most of his sons continued in his lifestyle. However, his wife may have received her revenge as she went to play golf when his stroke hit. She told the staff to let him rest.

World War II took Joseph's eldest son, the one he was grooming for the presidency. Another daughter was killed in a plane crash. Joseph refused to give her a proper Catholic burial because she was married to a non-Catholic, and her brother, Joseph, Jr., was the only one to attend the funeral. So much power, yet so much insanity.

Abraham Lincoln suffered from guilt that grew into insanity. After his dearest son, Willie, died, he went to his grave and had him exhumed to see and touch him again. Embalming was a relatively new procedure at that time. Mrs. Lincoln took the death of her son even harder than Abraham and remained bedridden for a long time. She was described as being a schizophrenic after her death.

J. Edgar Hoover led a truly bizarre life. His mother was his world but he'd be so angry as she continually warned him of homosexuals, begging him not to be a "daisy." He was cross-dressing from an early age, and couldn't help but wear his mother's clothes and jewelry while dancing around his room.

Hoover was a pathological liar, claiming to be with the G-men who took credit for taking out criminals like Baby-Face Nelson, Bonnie and Clyde, etc. Hoover was actually in his office writing a fake biography, even though he was director of the FBI at the time. He was a narcissist, loving power and attention. Thriving on having something against presidents, including Truman and Nixon, their wives and anyone else in politics, he hid his private life.

Hoover was also a sociopath, believing he could do no wrong. Believing he was the most powerful man in the country, he never cared or thought about other people's lives. Unlike Kennedy, he did not drink to excess to soothe himself, but his life partner said Hoover overused medication from the beginning of their relationship.

FDR (Franklin Roosevelt) was also a narcissist. To be fair, it must take that type of personality to want to be leader of the free world. He honestly believed the American public didn't know he was wheelchair bound, just as JFK hid his illnesses, as more examples of their pathological lying. They believed their power allowed them any woman they wanted.

Lyndon Johnson believed he was all-powerful as a senator. As a psychopath, his social behavior in his hatred of the Kennedy family and his behavior as President became appalling. He felt so important and powerful that he'd hang onto his penis when issuing orders. He urinated on the Whitehouse lawn every day, and would gladly swing around at a urinal showing off his "jumbo" penis. He was a heavy drinker and felt he was abused and abandoned, and was upset when he did not run for re-election.

As we know from history, Richard Nixon had multiple problems: narcissism, psychopathic and sociopathic. He talked to portraits in the White House. He blamed everyone else for anything and tried to destroy evidence in the Watergate investigation and others. Currently we have a president, Trump, who, if you watch old Nixon tapes, has him hands-down in crazy behavior. He destroys policies and laws out of jealousy without understanding what he is doing. He's the first president to say, "I'm very intelligent. Very, very much a genius, and the most sane person there is anywhere." Wow!

We've skipped many people. The younger generation of stars, musicians, etc. have had their own terrifying episodes of suicides and murders. Perhaps the new trend of "alternate truth" and "verbally assaulting" people will only escalate mental illness across the country and there will be no stopping alternate opioids and other drugs to keep going for as long as they can.

Yes, our country is in trouble, but in getting rid of opioids without providing widespread availability of mental health clinics and hospitals, other addictions will take over. In a few years, a new pharmaceutical drug will be blamed as the worst problem in the United States.

Problems in any country are not because of a new musical trend such as Rock and Roll, which was disparaged with Elvis' hip movement to Michael's crotch grabbing to Snoop Dog's language, or go way back to Frank Sinatra and screaming bobbysoxers waiting by his stage door. Yes, there were drugs that were problems even then. Prescription abuse of diet pills, aka speed, was rampant due to body image shaming. Valium with the evening cocktail blurred many angry newlyweds. We're told to give our children medication to keep them sitting in a straight line, just like everyone else in the class. We need to find out who is in trouble due to mental illness rather than blaming drugs and medications to hide the real problems being covered up and untreated. Then, people who physically require a proper painkiller will have the ability to get the appropriate prescriptions for their real pain. People who actually need a psychiatrist or therapist will have their needs met as well. This will be the cure to the "Opioid Crisis" in America.

We will be spending time discussing various situations, including our own. All of the information included in this book is true from personal experience or surveys and conversations/interviews and assorted news articles. There can be no claim of slander, libel or defamation from anything written here. Names may or may not be changed depending on the circumstances.

Shall we begin?

DID

October 21, 2017

As of today, these are my diagnosis: DID (Dissociative Identity Disorder/Multiple Personalities), PTSD (Post-Traumatic Stress Disorder), Severe Anxiety, Social Anxiety, and Undiminished Depression.

I've been diagnosed and mistreated with bi-polar disease in 2016, when the psychiatrist/nursing psychiatrist was considering using shock treatments because the medications didn't work. They made me vague and sick or hyper and paranoid. I was given a strong medication for schizophrenia. They didn't tell me the sun would blister your skin with this. I found out.

I was always anxious; couldn't do anything without someone, anyone, to give me permission; and I was told that I had ADHD in 1983. By having multiples, I'm often doing more than one thing. In 1997 Adderall was administered after the diagnosis. The drug actually helped in being able to be "me," in focus more often. I still take it: 15 mg in the morning and again at noon. I was labeled to be a compulsive liar in the 1970s in the Singer Center in Rockford, Illinois. My mom gave them the diagnosis and told them I'd had it for years. She said it had been genetically passed down from my biological mother. So I was pulled off schizophrenia meds without tapering them. My legs hurt so badly from this and I screamed for weeks in the mornings until I could get stretched enough to move without pain.

In the 1980s a psychiatrist in California was beginning to bring up child abuse. I told him that they (my adoptive parents) didn't love me but that was because I was so bad. I couldn't sleep during this time and took a green capsule: chloral hydrate, I think.

I was diagnosed with anxiety when I started running out of stores because people made me so nervous. I took 5 mg of Valium B.I.D. from the same doctor in California.

I've found myself in hospitals and doctors' offices and not knowing how, what, where, why. Given loads of drugs: Geodon, Prednisone. I was given Phenobarbital by a psychiatrist in Missouri. I was forgetting who I was, my son, where I was, then would get a huge headache and pass out. I was too sleepy to function. An MD gave me Geodon and I slept constantly. I had to put my son in a temporary "boy's home." This was combined with the Phenobarbital and Restoril prescribed by same doctor and he knew I was on the Phenobarbital. By now it is 1998 or 1999 and all I did was sleep. Finally, I went to a Mental Health Clinic; then with an inpatient facility in Mexico, Missouri called The Arthur Center. It's still there, but no inpatient is a problem EVERYWHERE.

I met Dr. Imram Chishti at the Arthur Center. He met with me for one hour every week for three weeks and said he had a diagnosis. Dissociative Identity Disorder (DID) was very rare and he wanted me to allow him to admit me to the Arthur Center for a month. I went. Now he practices in Chesterfield, Missouri.

Dr. Chishti got me started with medicines, therapy, hypnosis, and sleep C-pap. He was moving and gave me to the best doctor at the Arthur Center. I was with him weekly for three years. He called me every night to make sure that my son and my alters and I were ok. He moved to New Zealand for a few years, but now practices in Missouri.

The next "doctor" was in Pueblo, Colorado. He thought I was demon-possessed and kept trying to exorcise me. He thought my demons had jumped into my son, too. So he also tried to exorcise him. I was physically ill at this time of my life. It was a HORRIFYING experience. I have no idea how long this went on, but it was close to a year. They decided I was too evil to be "exorcised." I haven't entered a church since!

I found a clinic with a good therapist. I had the same medicine from Dr. Hall and in a group, too. Then we moved back to Missouri. I went back to the Arthur Center. The first psychiatrist wouldn't treat me for DID because she hadn't diagnosed me. The second called Family Services for everything. No medications were dispensed. The third psychiatrist sort of believed me and gave me a couple of low doses. He wanted me to travel to Columbia for a day-long test to see if I might have DID. The application was 25 pages long. I couldn't do it. I saw him for a while though.

I found a general practitioner who gave me the medications I needed. A niece stole a bottle of Klonopin and at the next month doctor's visit they had me take a urine test. No Klonopin in my system. I hadn't filled out a police report, so no more doctor. The same niece called Family Services and told them I was giving drugs to my son. They came and found that my son didn't live with me. He was in Paris, Missouri and I hadn't seen him in a month and one week. That was the end of Family Services, but my niece didn't wait long enough and thought I'd called a mutual friend about Social Services coming.

She said, "Oh, Auntie, are you okay? What happened?"

I said, "What are you talking about? I'm just fine."

She tried saying, "Tish told me..." since I hadn't spoken with Tish. I never spoke with her again.

Then I watched my life go to hell in a hand basket. Spinning out of control. I couldn't stop it. I knew, but I couldn't do anything. My son was back living with me, angry with me and everyone else.

DID 2005-2006 Exorcism

I'd been working with two psychiatrists treating me for DID for six years of weekly therapy, with seven hospitalizations in the psychiatric hospital with which they were affiliated, sometimes at the clinic three or four times a week to talk to the on-call emergency staff. I would call the crisis line, sometimes ten times a day and other days none.

One of the doctors was the one who diagnosed me. He often admitted me to the hospital because so many memories that the alters had held all these years were slamming into me so quickly; others tried to protect me from the memories. I put my son, Rian, in a "Boys Family Ranch" for the first year of my treatment. The hardest thing I ever did in my life was to sign the guardianship of my little boy over to these people for one year. I felt like taking him and running away and just going on. But I knew I couldn't do it for either one of us. I didn't even get to visit him for a month. He seemed happy, healthy and enjoying living on a farm. He was the youngest one there, and received a lot of attention from his "big brothers."

Treatment and medication trials were the hardest work I'd ever done. I went through hypnosis. That helped the doctor know how many "people" he was dealing with. Some had such a tiny role and time in my life he was able to integrate; join them to me, then and there. He also shared their stories with me. By the time he was finished with hypnosis, I had 49 alters left out of the 109 I'd started with. No wonder I was so "scatter-brained." But this is not that story for now.

My first doctor had moved away, giving me to his partner. I said I wouldn't like him, but I did. He was absolutely great, just like I was told.

I'd been thinking of moving back to Colorado. My best friend was battling cancer for the fourth time. My son's god-parents were there, and I thought I'd just settle in with old, good friends. Because of discovering my mental illness, treatment and some physical illnesses that probably came from stress, I found that people act differently when you aren't the same. My friend died a month before we got there.

Before I left, and what helped me leave, was that my psychiatrist was moving to another country and my son's godparents had found me a psychiatrist who dealt with DID. It seemed as if all of my "ducks were in a row."

The ducks fell quickly.

Rian's godfather is a pastor. He and his wife had been my closest friends (or they wouldn't have been my son's godparents). When we flew into Denver, they met us at the airport and we were staying at their house for a month while finding a place to live. It was uncomfortable after a week.

Then they took me to meet the psychiatrist. It was in an old professional building. So far, so good. We got to his office and he and his wife were there together, a couple in their mid to late 70s. Very nice. We were given hot tea and all sat around a table in quilt-covered, comfy chairs.

Okay, a nice get-to-know-you meeting where Dr. "Crazy" began the meeting in prayer. And I thought *What the fuck is this about?* I really, really wanted to run for my life, but wasn't self-confident enough to go.

He told me his success rate in the past 30 years of eliminating all of the alters in people's lives. Those stories were impressive. Then he explained to me that alters were, in themselves, evil. Fear pounded in my chest, my head hurt and I knew I was leaving so one of my alters (saviors) could deal with this conversation. They'd obviously dealt with alters before because, according to the clock, they got me back in about 15 minutes. They prayed again that I would stay present and in charge throughout the session. I was doing the things my psychiatrists had taught me: non-verbally asking them to let me go through this session, give them permission to stay close, listen and write their thoughts about this when we left. Then I kept my focus on Dr. Crazy's tie so he'd think I was looking at him, while I was repeating to myself, "I am Cheri Fetter-Jimenez. I am. I am. I am. No one will ever damage me again." All of this was in my head while they were talking.

He was a doctor with a PhD in religion and a BA in counseling. SHIT!

He started explaining angels to me, their rank and job descriptions. Then he talked about Satan's angels. They were all sneaky, devious and ready to step in to every situation we weren't able to handle. Child abuse was one of their favorite times to invade a person's life. They were able to do this whether we were Christians or non-believers. He assumed (making an ass of both of us!) that I was a Christian because of my relationship with the godparents. I didn't contradict him, yet I don't know why!?!

Apparently the treatment Dr. "Crazy" had in mind was exorcism. Like Marlena on *Days of Our Lives* and the girl with a spinning head spewing pea soup . . . I knew about exorcism. Holy shit! That would have been better. Tie me to a fucking bed and see if I could levitate shit, come and go, burn me with holy water and let me scream and growl while they read the Bible. But, no, this was going to be done one alter at a time.

I'd been naïve enough to bring highlights and several letters of my treatment to date, giving them to Dr. Crazy. He said he would read through them and we would meet in one week. He asked me if I minded if my son's godparents were there. Foolishly, I thought they'd jump in if there was any weirdness. He gave me a list of scripture to read. I'd read the Bible several times, so I scanned the headings: "Jesus cast out demons in a crowd:" "Jesus casts out demons without having to be with the person;" "The disciples cast out demons." The disciples aren't able to cast out demons…Jesus told them that they needed to pray and fast before dealing with the hard ones. And "Jesus gives a parable about cleaning a house and because it's not filled and the door shut it gets seven times worse. Then Jesus Christ explains when you cast out a demon you must put him inside and guard the door with and angel." Dr. Crazy said it was a warrior angel, 10 feet tall and armed to fight. I didn't see that anywhere. Maybe that came from one of those prophecy books that made your brain leak?

And then it was time for "The Appointment." Same round table, quilts on the chairs, Crazy doc was on one side and my son's godfather, the pastor, was on the other. Their wives were across from me. The room seemed kind of dim and it was too hot. I asked for cold water.

Of course, everyone held hands to pray. There was a lot of asking God to put the big-assed angels around us and to guard the door. Then he prayed that the comforting angels surround me and then loving angels to fill the room. That room was pretty crowded by now. It was hot, even though the heat had been turned down. Of course, as Crazy prayed, the pastor added his prayers and the wives said, "Amen, yes, Lord and thank you." I said nothing and just looked around.

Then the praying became extremely bizarre. Crazy was speaking to Satan, "binding him from action by the blood of Jesus, telling him he had no authority in this room, nor did his servants, the demons. He told Satan that they were going to be binding the demons and throwing them into the pit of hell where they'd wait for the day when the same thing would be done to him."

Unfortunately, they weren't finished. One of my triggers for PTSD (Post-traumatic Stress Disorder) was this type of religion. Finally, that was so bad that one of my alters who I knew as Elizabeth, was out and I was protected by her.

Dr. Hall from Missouri had trained them to write about their experiences so I wouldn't miss so many parts of my life. This is what poor Elizabeth suffered according to her letter:

"The two men put oil on my forehead. They were speaking in tongues. What we consider as a fake language will be talked about later on in Cheri's story. Then they asked me my name. I told them I was Elizabeth. They wanted to know how old I was. I said 20. That's because that's when I came to help Cheri. The doctor thanked me for coming to help her, and said I needed to go. Well, I told them I couldn't until Cheri said so and that we had a psychiatrist to help us. He said we didn't need a psychiatrist because we had god and all of his angels to help us and keep us safe. He said my name was written in the "Lamb's Book of Life" and I would be in heaven forever. I told him I didn't want to go there. We knew we were bad and that I didn't want to talk anymore. They tried to get one of the invisible angels to take me. I never saw anything coming to take me. They said the pastor said god told him that "I was a stronghold and needed fasting and prayer." Everyone agreed. I didn't hear God, either.

They wanted Cheri to come back. I wasn't leaving her with these kooks! So, I stayed. I said Cheri could come back after we made sure her son was okay, and then took a nap. I didn't feel like answering any more questions. I didn't like them. So, we went to the pastor's and saw Rian and went to sleep. Then Cheri woke up with my letter tucked in her arm under the pillow."

I read Elizabeth's letter and wondered how I could get out of this mess. To make this brief, they talked to alter after alter and couldn't get them to leave. They started saying my son was moody because my demons were jumping into him. We talked all of the time and were thrilled to find a house to rent. He was really upset by what was happening to me. His godparents were talking to him without my knowledge. He knew about my alters before anyone else did. He grew up with them and knew they weren't demons.

Rian went to sessions with me and asked them to pray for him. He could have won an Oscar for his exorcism performance. I think my mouth was hanging open. The insane religious maniacs were so happy, leaping around and praising God. Rian fell asleep. They said that was normal. They made another appointment for me.

My son tried to teach me to fake it the way he did. I couldn't do it, mostly because alters were coming out every which way to protect me from that hot mess.

We started "missing" the pastor's church services on a regular basis. I was sick a lot, and my son was with made-up people.

The final conclusion about me was that I, not my alters, was inflicted with evil because I allowed it to my unrepentant evil. There was no way to free me from the demons. But in the beginning they told the alters they hadn't done anything wrong. They thanked them for helping me with all of the things I'd been through. They even offered to send them to heaven, but now they were called "demons" that were there because of my evilness, and that until I repented and confessed before God and man I was too evil to free.

This process went on for about three months. It left me with an angry son, exhausted and knowing that I never would be inside a church again in my life! My son struggled through every minute of school until I pulled him out and put him in an online school. It was run by churchie types, but harmless. He also ended up in some anger management classes. I found a real psychiatrist and therapist. We moved away without contacting the godparents.

They caught my son online. He told them I was dead. Atta Boy! He called his godfather shortly afterwards. When we got to Colorado, he'd been told by his godfather that he was stepping up to be his dad and that he would be the same as his children in his life, etc., etc., but they never invited him to family swims at some club. He'd pick him up to come over after he'd taken his sons to ride derby cars, etc…etc…then they tried to take him away from me while I was hospitalized with double pneumonia for the third time in three months. I was listening to my son talk to this lying sack of shit. He said: "I want to thank you for being just like my dad. You were. You lied, left me out, and hurt my mom. So, yes, you were exactly like my dad!" He hung up. What a great kid!

I'm guessing they still think I'm dead, and obviously don't give a shit about the godson they made promises to in a religious service at their church when my son was about two years old. I pick godfathers out as well as I pick out husbands. The cure for that is to quit!

DID 2014 – Story from a nursing home

One of my friends I met in the first nursing home (June, 2014) was bi-polar. Her daughter was also bi-polar and killed herself when she was only 17. My friend's ex-husband forced her to put their daughter into a grade school psychiatric in-care, lifetime home. This happened near St. Louis, Missouri. The ex never saw their daughter again, and after a year of his sleeping on the couch and barely speaking to my friend, one day he just didn't come home from work. They divorced about three to four months later. She lived on disability. He didn't pay her anything even though he was supposed to according to the divorce.

My friend, who I'll call "M" ended up moving in with her mother and who knows how many cats. M had been in and out of psych hospitals all of her life, including a couple of year-long periods. As an adult she worked 15 years as a bookkeeper, but had to take time off for periods in the hospital; the longest time missed was two months

When M was about eight years old, her mother started to notice that she wasn't "quite right." She'd go from kind and loving to shrieking and kicking to sleeping all of the time and refusing to leave her dark room and then became hyperactive, unable to sit still, stop talking or doing the same "chore" over and over. It was happening constantly so she took M to the family doctor. He recommended a psychiatrist.

M's mom was ashamed about taking her little girl to "a place like that" and didn't take for three months. She never told any other family members.

They admitted M to the hospital. This place had no other children. M was scared of everything and everyone. So she quit eating and cried all of the time.

After the first week, without a diagnosis, she was given her first shock treatment. It was 1960. M remembers being in a white room with an older nurse who was kind along with the doctor. She was terrified of him. She said he had a huge nose, filled with hairs and little buggers. Gross! They put wires on her head at first, shaving little patches of her hair! That's when she started to cry. Then they gave her a shot, of who knows what.

M thinks she started "being alive again" (her words) four days later. She stuttered, dropped things and forgot simple things like wearing shoes. But, she was happy and calm and she wasn't afraid. M started playing checkers with a couple of residents and ate and slept well. Her mom came and got her three days later.

This pattern repeated itself until M was 15 years old. Her mom found a better psychiatric doctor in a new office and made the change. M said her mother saw her becoming less and less of who M was. M didn't notice but knew that something was wrong with and wondered if she'd die from "it."

M thinks this may have been when they said she was bi-polar, but thinks it had a different name for the same thing (most likely manic-depressive). It was about 1975. M went to school, dances, and learned to crochet and sew They gave her pills: one kind for when she was sad, another for each symptom. When she felt good, she didn't take her medicine, so she ended up in the hospital in 1977 until 1978. And she was given shock treatments during the entire year, sometimes more often than others. M told me the medicine did awful things to her. She had dry mouth so she could barely speak. Another felt as if she was being held down in bed. This was for hyper periods. She felt old. Her skin was dry and her teeth loose. Her menstrual cycle was all month or none.

She begged and begged her mom to get her out, and finally she did, with a bunch of different medicines for every symptom. M still only took randomly due to the side-effects.

Even though she never felt "normal" or even knew what it was, that was all she wanted. So she met her husband, a friend of a cousin's son. She thought he was kind and quiet and so they got married. Her daughter was born a little over a year later. They were married at the Justice of the Peace. Her mom bought her a new hat. They went to her husband's friend's hunting cabin for three days and two nights. He only brought sandwiches and coffee.

M had a major downswing episode when the baby was just a month old. Of course, they didn't have any idea of post-partum depression. That probably exacerbated her bi-polar disease.

She spent a month in the hospital. Her mom took care of the baby. Her husband ignored the whole thing and acted like nothing ever happened.

So years passed. She was divorced, lived with her mom and spent one day a year with her "hospitalized" daughter. From the description of the house she and her mom lived in, it was one step away from being condemned, or maybe it was. There was no working furnace, so they shared a room with twin beds and a space heater. Her mom was bedridden. M couldn't really remember why. They didn't have hot water. M was tired after work, so they ate soup or sandwiches. They kept peanut butter and bread in the bedroom so her mom had lunch. Her mom died and she lost the house and her job, but she fed all the cats that came around. Six lived inside, and she still worries about them.

After a three-month stint in another psychiatric hospital, she was put in a nursing home. M said she didn't mind being there. Her medication kept being changed and increased. She was sent to the psychiatric hospital again about two years after being at the home, and once again had shock treatments.

The nursing home decided she was too difficult to take care of and found a place for her in Troy, Missouri, north by at least fifty miles, and she'd never been there. I met her shortly after I went to Troy Manor. She was a little weird, but, who isn't? We didn't talk much about our personal lives, sat at the same Bingo table, and went to activities together sometimes. She went to psychiatric hospitals two times while I was there for eight months.

She got very jealous over anyone I'd ever talked to. It got so bad that I just was rude until she left me alone (I'm just wonderful – good thing I never finished nursing school).

After a friend of mine passed away, I wanted to move and went to Silex, Missouri to another home. Then, about three months after I'd been at Silex, M arrived. She was in a wheelchair and didn't remember me at all.

So I wheeled her to her room after lunch. I talked her into a few "activities" and one day she said: "I know you. You're my friend." She eventually graduated to a cane.

During this time she told me about her life. She was very "clingy" and wanted me to take care of her, fight her battles, and more. She told me that she came to Silex after the psychiatric hospital. She'd tried to kill herself and had to go. In thirty days she had seventy shock treatments. It was a creepy, weird hospital in the ghetto of St. Louis. I went there once for three days. I felt it was the 1800s . . . really awful!

I would notice her cycling periods and try to alert the staff. M often threatened suicide, sometimes stupidly like: "I'm going to drink the water in the mop bucket if you don't let me go to the hospital."

She was so upset when I told her I was moving to Columbia. At first she was determined to come with me. I used everything I could think of to change her mind. I convinced her by saying I needed to go first and get used to everything so I could help her when she came. In the meantime, we could call and write each other. So, I helped her get a cell phone, and by some miracle I didn't kill her during the three weeks I spent teaching her how to use it!

After I left, she went directly to a psychiatric hospital. She wrote me a letter a day. It was getting creepy because she kept telling me how much she loved me. And she called at 5 a.m. or midnight or any time. If I didn't answer my cell phone, she'd call the front desk.

Silex wouldn't take her back. The place they found her sounded like a dump, with eight people to a room. I wrote her once in awhile. I also convinced her that I would call her every Saturday at 1 p.m. It worked for awhile. Then she went to another psychiatric hospital and more shock treatments. Then a different home, one that was a little better. She couldn't remember anything, but called me in every cycle. I felt like I was being stalked. Having my own psychological issues, I couldn't take care of her, and I got her to stop. Sometimes I feel very sad about that.

One of the things she used to say to me was: "In my whole life, all I did was fall through the cracks." Me too, for a long time. Most of us probably feel that way when our minds are sick.

M's daughter got the court to let her out of the psychiatric care home. M said she was able to act very mature and charming at times. She went to be near her mom. M never explained to me why she only saw her once a year. Apparently her daughter didn't hold a grudge. Or, it was all she knew and had no way to compare it to other families outside of the facility.

The daughter was very promiscuous and was usually with older men. She believed she was a "black magic witch." She scared people into giving her money, clothes, places to live and whatever she wanted. M loved her so much. M was an old-fashioned, speaking in tongues kind of Christian. he believed her daughter would be saved with enough prayer. It sounded like M dragging her to church was their only disagreement.

They both cycled through their bi-polarism, and rarely were in the same cycle at the same time. On top of everything, it made them co-dependent on each other. M had been very depressed and wanted to go to the hospital. She wanted shock treatments because she felt as if the medicines were killing her. She had a big fight with her daughter. A day and a half later, the police came and took her to identify her 17-year-old. She'd put a gun to her head. The man who owned the apartment and gun was long gone. M doesn't know how long she was in the psych ward afterwards. She told me this with absolutely NO EMOTION in her voice or any type of body language, nor did she react that I was sobbing by the end of the story. She thanked me for staying to listen.

Now I'm stuck in a nursing home where the administrative and some of the other staff bully me for my mental illness.

A Tale of Three Alters

****Note: It is important to understand that the alter personalities in a patient with DID will often be aware of what is happening to the actual person, and will integrate what is happening to the "host" within their own existences. Most people with DID have four to fifteen alter personalities, but there are cases of more than 100 personalities of varying ages, gender and can even be animals.**

Here are three stories from alter personalities of one person with DID. These stories were written by each alter; however the actual person believes and has some memories of the happenings. Often times the alters will totally hide events from the person, but these things are usually brought out in therapy by hypnosis and fills in the blank spaces of time (amnesia) that the patient has had during their lifetime. The alters usually appear to the patient during times of stress or traumatic events. Often times different alters will protect the patient at the same time, and will offer very similar stories of specific events, but there are enough differences to show that each personality has its own identity with separate viewpoints about a situation. Each can have their own family history, so it can become extremely confusing to the patient once they become aware of their diagnosis. It is extremely difficult for friends and family to understand the circumstances of DID. Even for psychiatrists, the usual minimum amount of time to diagnose DID. is 7 years.

#1 Childhood physical and mental abuse

One of the worst memories I have of my mother acting "crazy" happened when I was seven years old. It was raining outside and she was watching two of the neighbor's kids. Because they were there, she brought out a game, my little record player and records. Little kid records, 78 rpm: "Turkey in the Straw," "Three Blind Mice," "Twinkle, Twinkle Little Star," and others.

We were playing in the basement. There was a nice little area to play in with lots of room with a little table and chairs.

We were playing my records and singing along, jumping around and laughing, especially at the blackbirds in a pie . . . whatever song that was. "Old King Cole" comes to mind.

Suddenly, my mom was down there. She had a slip on. You could see her girdle and the garters holding up one stocking. The other one was hanging on her legs. She had black hairs on her legs and under her arms. She put "Turkey in the Straw" on and said: "Come on kids, let's dance!"

She made us join hands and started us moving in a circle. Singing at the top of her voice, she didn't have a voice that ever hit the right notes. She put the record on again. This time we were moving in a circle, but she was kicking her legs as far as they could go in the air. I think all of our mouths were open. She was pretty overweight, which didn't help my embarrassment. Then she put a marching song on and we were suddenly following her around the basement. She was high-stepping, clapping and singing. I don't think the record had words. She did, rhyming bizarre words like glad, mad, sad, bad, had…up, cup, sup, pup…etc., etc. She was laughing a very scary laugh. Then she stopped marching, singing and rhyming and started crying and ran upstairs.

A few minutes later she put a tray on the steps and yelled "lunch." It seemed okay. Peanut butter and jelly sandwiches, but there were ten of them and three of us. A tiny bowl of Fritos with five corn chips and six paper cups of chocolate milk, and those gummy candies I hated. It had a green orange, red, yellow and black; that's all I remember. She knew I hated them! They were called "Chuckles." There were also two Fudgesicles with a note that they were for my two friends. There was a half of an orange Popsicle with a note with huge letters: FAT GIRL.

None of us had spoken a word since she'd first come to the basement. My neck and face were hot so I know I was embarrassed and bright red. Finally, one of my friends put an arm around me and said, "We will never talk about this again…to each other or anyone else. And maybe we'll forget." My other friend her put her arm around me on the other side. She said to "spit on our hands and mix them up." We did and this is a lifetime pinkie swear! We hooked our three pinkies together and said "We swear to keep this secret forever."

Fifty-four years later I'm breaking the pact. It is an illuminating vision of my mom's psychopathic behavior. By the time we ate lunch, we carefully went upstairs with the tray and leftover food. None of us liked "Chuckles."

My mom was on the phone, fully dressed, having a regular conversation with a friend. Regular tone of voice; no evidence of hysteria or jumping around. I passed her a note to see if we could watch "Felix the Cat" and either "Batman" or "Superman." "Batman" might not have been on TV yet. She nodded "yes" and we went to the living room to watch television. My friends' moms came for them one at a time, and I had to turn off the TV. Then I had to bring up the game, records and record player because she kept most of my stuff in her closet so I couldn't play.

I now need to let you know that I was adopted. It is important for many reasons, as I learned that growing up I had two moms that didn't want me. Finding out that my birth mom was actually my favorite aunt affected me greatly, especially since she wouldn't tell her husband that

I was his daughter, but my half-sisters got a stepdad who was wonderful! I had to keep that from my "uncle."

My adoptive mother had all the traits of a psychopath. She had tons of instances of displays of abnormal behavior besides what I described. She made plans with people then left home when they were supposed to be there, and would call them screaming and yelling horrible things because they didn't come over.

She directed moderate violence to my dad almost daily. Nothing he did was good enough. She thought nothing of yelling a screaming at him: at home or in a restaurant or someone else's house. For whatever reason, he put up with her until he died at age 61.

Her most violent behavior was to me. I'll be writing more about it, at length. She would stick bottles, crochet hooks and other things up my vagina for as long as I can remember. I have a clear memory of her lowering the side of my crib to molest me. She seemed to get pleasure from punching me hard enough to make me lose my breath or to cause a nose bleed. It made her laugh.

She was involved at church, a wife of one of the "pastors" and performed her role perfectly. She was involved in school activities, room mother, PTA and everywhere else there was a need.

Sometimes she had terrible headaches. She said she'd be a good person if she didn't have such pain. Other times, most times, her behavior was all my fault. I was so bad. She told me I was a "punishment from God." I ruined her life and made her behave in ways that she couldn't stop. If she could beat me to death, her life would be so happy.

Then I watched her with other people. A boy in my class, all through grade school, had diabetes. This horrible woman always brought him sugar-free candy and soda for parties. She brought gallons of soup to families going through sickness, death or hard times. One of her friend's daughters was laid up in a body cast for three months. My mom took her a gift, usually a craft for her to do, every single day.

She hid her psychopathy from the entire "normal" part of the world except for the day with my friends. But, she also belonged to a coven of evil, evil people and all of them were able to release their craziness.

I believe my grandmother had problems as well. She was a very cold woman. When she was young she spent a lot of times in "speak-easys." The next day her room would have the black-out shades down and would be suffering from a sick headache. Her daughters walked on tip-toes on those days.

After her first husband died she took in boarders to pay the bills. According to my aunt, she started sleeping with one of her boarders fairly soon after her husband died. She shared a room with the girls. They shared the big bed and their mom had a smaller bed near them. My aunt said that most mornings she woke up because the bedroom door would open. She'd watch her mother put a robe on over her naked body and then mess up the covers on the small bed. They eventually married and she had three more children. Her second husband died before they were teens.

She practiced a religion that believed you could contact the dead at will and that they would guide you. They practiced a mix of white and black magic. We never ate a meal at her house. She never hugged us, but we were told to kiss her whenever we'd been together. She had no interest in her grandchildren at all. It didn't sound as if she cared about her children, either.

She was a seamstress after her second marriage and for the rest of her life. She resented the rich women and their fancy clothes, coats and hats that she altered, fitted and hats and stoles from the extra material so they would pay extra.

When I was a kid, one of my punishments was to be locked in the basement. One of the first things I found was a box full of pictures, letters, postcards and documents of a little girl, Esther. By reading every-thing I found out a few things. One of her aunts addressed mail to her using their maiden last name. Other letters and documents used a last name I'd never heard of. Esther was sick and in a hospital too far away for her mom to come every day. She had my mom, a baby and my aunt, a little bit older to take care of at home. Esther was in grade school. Her classmates and teachers sent dozens and dozens of post cards to her. She died at the hospital. It didn't sound as if she had any family with her. She was so pretty with blond curly hair and bright blue eyes. This was portrayed in a couple of photos that had been "colorized" in the style of the day. Lots of times I felt as if she was there, waiting for me to pull out the pictures and letters so we could play together. There are still times I feel her presence near me. She is happy and content: forever a beloved child. Sometimes I am jealous and I feel her say: "It's okay, I love you."

The next box had pictures of a good-looking guy with a really awesome car: a convertible, two-toned, with wheels just like the car on each side. My grandmother was young and very pretty. She had nice clothes and gorgeous hats. The pictures would have both of their full names on the back.

Under the pictures was an old cigar box. Inside of it were papers showing that my grandmother married that man. Then she gave birth to Esther. Before Esther was born they were divorced. It had to be sometime in the 1800s. They were divorced because my grandmother committed adultery.

From letters, I discovered that her father allowed her to move back home. The pictures of the house looked like it was a nice place: really big with a huge wrap-around porch. Wicker furniture and big beautiful ferns were on the porch. There was a gazebo, a garden and lots of flowers.I guess my grandmother was living in the servants' quarters and working with them. Her father didn't speak to her. Even years later, he rarely spoke to her. Her mother helped her knit and sew for the baby and always "pleaded her situation" with her father.

Grandmother's sister and father wanted her to give the baby to her sister. It didn't make sense. She was a single woman all of her life. She also had beautiful clothes, hats and jewelry. In the letters between the sisters there were hateful accusations and remarks. I guess her sister had moved away and had an affair with a married man. Grandma threatened to tell their dad unless she dropped the adoption issue. She must have done so. She had the affair for over 30 years until he died. She travelled a lot, alone or with friends. That way she could vacation with her "man" without anyone finding out.

When their father died years after their mother, they had to sell the house and most of the things in it to pay their father's debts. Their letters sounded as if every step was a battle between the sisters. Grandma got into the house first and took everything she wanted, leaving her sister very angry: a "tradition" I've seen pass through 3 generations, counting theirs.

I didn't interpret all of this as a kid. Once I'd moved away and came back for visits, I'd bring a box upstairs and ask question after question. This made my mother angry and then she'd cry because I was so mean wanting to know about it all. I was used to her tantrums, so I kept going. It was my history and I wanted to know. It looked as if my great-grandfather had problems of being judgmental, controlling and cruel.

My grandmother was a bit of a slut and seemed to lie easily. She considered men to be more important than her children. She had a lot of anger that was held in, and absolutely was unable to be affectionate to her children or grandchildren. I think she and her father were sociopaths, and produced my mom, a psychopath, and I ended up with DID, with Post-Traumatic Stress Disorder, anxiety, social anxiety and non-treatable depression. Gee thanks, you guys. Not exactly a family tree with Mary Poppins as the mom!

My older sister and younger brother were spared the "crazy gene" and have had pretty regular lives, in their own styles. We're fairly close and I know that they didn't have the life I did. I'm glad of that. One in a family is more than enough!

I think my entire reason for being their daughter was to have someone to involve in their secret satanic lives. And my mom just enjoyed beating on me or hurting me at every opportunity she had. I think she loved my sister and brother. Even now, with so much therapy and real help along with the right medication I finally received, I still will have a thought that I was punished because I am a horrible person and unworthy to be treated well. DID folks have trouble ridding ourselves of all of our life-messages, but we can call for help or talk ourselves through with the right therapy and medication.

#2 Childhood Delivery

I have DID, PTSD, anxiety and depression. To the outside world our family was "normal." My sister Debbie was ten years older than I was, and my little brother was seven years younger than me. My dad was a preacher and my mom was always busy as a preacher's wife. Who could ask for better parents?

My mom did a lot of volunteer work at the school, at least when I was in grade school and later for my brother Randy. I guess she did for Debbie, but we were never at the same school. Deb didn't play much with us. She had a hi-fi, a boyfriend and a job. Sometimes she babysat, put the TV on and talked on the phone, but I thought she was so cool. I'll never forget the smell of Cover Girl make-up.

Both of my parents singled me out for torture. Preachers and their wives make a great cover for Satanic Cults and worshippers. I think they only had me for their sick, horrible rituals and their sick demented entertainment. Neither my sister nor brother was ever involved in my life of terror. I know they both thought they were hypocrites and mean people, but they've led regular lives and the little pieces of my life that I've shared are all things they don't know anything about. I'm very happy for that. We are closer as we've grown up, and I'm the only crazy one and probably have been for as long as they can remember.

One of the earliest memories I have is the side of my crib being lowered. I'm sure at the time all I knew was pain. Eventually I knew that my mom was putting all kinds of things up my vagina: crochet hooks, fingers, coke bottles with and without the metal tops, pens, letter openers and who knows what else.

She screamed at me all of the time. I was told I was stupid, fat, and no one could ever love a thing like me! I can still hear her voice telling me those things 20 years after she died. She hit me in the head, a lot. I'm sure that's why I have a headache every day. She broke my nose a couple of times and told the doctor it was from baseball. She made sure every grown-up I was around knew how "clumsy" I was. That explained all kinds of bumps and bruises.

She fed me DeCon rat and mice poison on top of my ice cream like sprinkles. I didn't realize that until my first husband and I had a mouse that could steal the cheese or lick the peanut butter and spring the trap. So, we got DeCon. When I opened it, some of the blue-green pieces fell out. My husband found me curled up in our closet with a blanket on top of me. I didn't know why.

I'd been going to psychiatrists since I was 18, but had never been given the right diagnosis or treatment. My life was a secret. My parents made it abundantly clear that if I ever told anyone one single thing about my life they would kill me. I had to reason not to believe them. I'd seen them and their cult members murder brand new babies – mine included. I watched one girl a year older than me beaten to death for talking to a teacher. A couple of girls disappeared.

Besides my mother torturing me every chance she had, there were the coven gatherings. Most of them took place in a church. There were people I knew and many I didn't. Always a circle of thirteen men. Women were clothed and unclothed, and then us, the girls. My introduction to this was at age nine. Debbie didn't live at home any more, and my brother went to sleep-overs all of the time.

The girls, including me, were raped over and over. I guess by each of the 13 men. There were rituals, incantations, candles, incense (the worst I've ever smelled – probably rotten bones lit on fire). I became pregnant the first time when I was 10 years old. I'd gotten my period that summer and my birthday is in January. I gave birth at a coven in another city. They had meetings there sometimes. My mother made sure I was always fat, so no one would know I was pregnant. When it was my 8th month, March, I went to relatives or friends or something for Easter and stayed to help with their kids. At least that's what my school knew. I did all of my homework and kept my grades up with A's.

When I gave birth, the circle of 13 was around me. They were the ones I knew. The women were there. I guess labor was long enough to give everyone time to get to their places.

Unfortunately, or quite possible fortunately, I don't have memories of my own about this. My brain had already split into Dissociative Identity Disorder, and I had a "crew" of alter personalities taking care of all of the worst parts of my life. After I was diagnosed with DID through hypnosis and writing, all of the gaps in my life were filled in. Each session was a horrible piece of memory. No matter how hard I tried to deny it, memories came back into my possession, little by little, as the alters decided I was ready. Not the psychiatrist. He suggested and helped and was there for me, sometimes 24/7; but the alters never stopped being in charge of protecting me.

Anyway, my mother took my baby girl and laid her on an altar in front of my father wearing his purple and black silky robe with symbols down the back. Another man I knew, a doctor in his other life, Dr. Ivan …., handed my father a silver knife that he'd taken out of an ornate silver sheath. They were all chanting and praying to Satan. My mother propped me up so I could see my father slicing my daughter's head off, and they made her into soup. All of the "new moms, including me, were forced to swallow some. If you threw up, you had to eat your vomit. That became a "thing" with my mother. Any time I ever got sick and vomited, I had to eat it. She enjoyed that a lot. Most people don't remember her smile or laugh. I do, but it wasn't anything that should be heard or seen.

#3 Raine

Raine is another protective alter of the same person as those mentioned above. During the interview, she was having problems learning how to use a smart phone because she had never been interested in new technology, so there were a few disconnects.

At the time of the interview, Raine had been "out" since the night before, as her host was so upset that the nursing home was trying to kick out a patient. They wanted to move her to another town because they say she (the patient) doesn't need a nursing home any longer now that her Hepatitis C has been cured. This woman is 63 and also has uncontrollable diabetes and encephalitis of a type that is a residual effect of the Hepatitis C. She could die of madness because her liver is so weak. At times she blanks out. Raine's host is concerned that the patient won't get good care, and does not feel that assisted living will give adequate care to her friend.

Raine's host will not be sent there, even though she is a better candidate for assisted living, as they feel that they are troublemakers together as friends. She feels as if she is being bullied by trying to separate them as friends. The two really depend on each other for emotional support. Most of the "professionals" at the nursing home do not understand DID, and avoid the patient most of the time due to their ignorance of the psychological illness.

The nursing home is in dire need of help. The nurses and aides are putting in 18-hour days because they are short-staffed. The head of nursing is afraid of DID because this disease has often been portrayed in movies such as "Sybil" and "The Three Faces of Eve." The staff has been instructed not to become friends with patients. Unfortunately for many of the patients, the only personal communication they receive is from the staff. Many have no families, were homeless, or do have families that have dropped them off never to be seen again.

Raine is aware that her host is not receiving adequate psychiatric help. The nursing home lost their one psychiatric aide, but that person was afraid of Raine's host, and would not allow her to go on customary outings, such as trips to Walmart. The supposed psychiatrist for the nursing home only pops her head in about once a month, looks at the medicines that are being given, and tells her she is doing fine. This takes about a total of two minutes. She doesn't even walk into the room, but simply pokes her head in the door. The nursing homes have their "blanket" psychiatrists, so the patients are not allowed to go to their own psychiatrists; however the host has been told that they are seeking transportation so that she can go see her old psychiatrist who diagnosed her many years ago. In the meantime, they don't want to deal with her and won't even allow her to call her prior psychiatrist.

Raine is urging her host to contact Tyler Perry, Oprah, Ellen or anyone who could spread awareness of DID and possibly offer monetary help to those in need. Patients are labeled once they enter the "system." The host has been in three nursing homes, and the current one is the worst of them all. Psychiatrists and medical doctors rarely visit, and nurses are only seen about once every four days. The aides deliver the medicines, and often they hand out the wrong ones to the wrong patients.

Mail is hard to get back and forth, as the aides must take them to the post office on their days off if it is something larger than a #10 envelope or a postcard. Raine comments that her host is such a sweet and giving person who is very creative and makes a lot of jewelry and artistic drawings that she always gives away. She never keeps any for herself, as she feels that she has no talent.

Raine is with her host at all times, and is aware of all that she encounters. She will come out to protect her host whenever she feels the need to withdraw from her current situation. She will allow the host to "rest" while Raine confronts the issues that are affecting her host's state of mind.

#4 And More

This particular person with DID has many alters. We have also had conversations with: Sandy, Elizabeth, Nick, Joey and a few others. They only come out to protect the host from stress. Although harmless, Nick has a tendency to cut the host's hair when he comes out. Another, who is a child, has a tendency to steal things when she is present, but will be happy to return items when asked.

Speaking with an Alter

As a layperson, it was very interesting for me to speak with an alter of someone diagnosed with DID. The alter's name is Zoe, and is one of the main "protectors" of the patient. She is very aware of the life of her physical host, and is thrilled with the idea that someone is writing about her/their lives.

She appeared to the patient, we will call her Grace, when she was about two years of age, yet Zoe was around twenty years of age and is fifty-nine at this time. She remained the age of twenty until Grace turned twenty. When young, Grace needed people to take care of her. Grace probably realized she was missing time before entering school, but not realizing that her alters existed until speaking with her therapist for many years.

Some of her alters have been with her a very long time, and two psychiatrists have concurred. Grace still is in conflict with making sense of her alters.

At present, Grace is in her 60s and in a nursing home, which is very bad for her. One of her caregivers is very good for her. Grace does have one brother, who she loves very much. She is existing because of Medicaid, and is only to keep $50 per month to buy assorted things she might want, such as peanut butter, ramen or drawing paper, art pencils and postage stamps. The food at the nursing home is of very poor quality. Even something as simple as grilled cheese is burnt so badly that it is inedible.

As a child, Grace started shoplifting. Influenced at a young age, at the age of eight she often had the psychological age of someone the age of four. She would steal because her mother taught the alter to steal and then blamed Grace. The mother would also hide items on Grace, influencing the tendencies to shoplift. The name of the young alter was Sarah, who is now integrated. According to Zoe, once an alter is integrated into a person, then what happened when the alter was active now becomes permanent memories. Grace's mother also took her to therapy, accusing her of being a liar and thief all of her life, so she was treated for that at a young age at an area institution.

Zoe feels badly that Grace has been bullied so much of her life in so many situations, and being in the nursing home at this time is not a good thing for Grace, as the nurses do not understand DID and think that Grace will turn into a killer if they aren't careful. That is not how DID works. Because of this, the staff members at the nursing home are afraid of her, and therefore, they will bully her. There have only been a few caregivers at the institution who have been kind to her. Others will not give her proper medication, using this as a form of punishment. Not only does Grace have DID, but she also has a few physical ailments, one of which requires monitoring of oxygen levels. There are times when the staff will not hook up the oxygen equipment when needed, or will hook it up, only to not turn on the oxygen!

Grace has had Zoe as a protector most of her life. Zoe was with her at each of Grace's suicide attempts, and was able to give her assistance when she was able. Other times, Grace was fortunate enough to be found in time, seemingly by coincidence. Zoe insists that writing and sketching for children's books are helping her from the formerly common appearance of so many alters, and that her newly reestablished relationship with her brother and his significant other of many years has given her hope for the future.

The suicide attempts were all brought about simply by being bullied, especially at work. Zoe keeps an eye on Grace all of the time, since the pattern of the day seems to be that it is acceptable to be rude, lie and that it is ok to be a bully. Since she is always with her, Zoe feels that Grace is doing very well now because she stays busy, especially drawing a lot for her few friends and family members. She is quite good at pencil drawings, and is going to attempt using pastels when she can afford them. On bad days, Zoe will get Grace to sleep for two or three days at a time.

Most of the suicide attempts were drug and alcohol related, but twice used cutting and once used a gun, but Grace's husband had taken his gun apart because he was concerned that she might harm herself or others. Grace thought she had put the gun together properly, but when she pulled the trigger it only clicked, so that attempt was foiled. That attempt was after all family came together in California, including her real mother, for the holidays, but nobody could tell her uncle who Grace's real mother was.

Another alter is Rain. She has a very laid back influence on Grace. Grace has a son who is in his 20s and has lived most of his life with a mother who has been in and out of institutions. They love each other very much, but because of his many years of living with a single mom (his father died from a drug overdose when he was quite young) with an unstable personality, he has difficulty coping with some normal daily activities. When Grace becomes frustrated with her son, Rain steps in and calms her down.

Zoe told me something very interesting. She believes that being punished for doing something good is a good way to turn someone into a bad person. I contemplated this statement, and I really believe that is true just from looking at my own past.

Zoe was especially concerned about the cult that Grace's mother and father embraced. Her mother would bring people from the coven to their house, and most of them also went to the church they attended. Zoe compared the cult to a Rainbow cult in Texas, but I could not find any information concerning a cult by that name that resembled Grace's family's cult. Zoe did confirm many of the stories of Grace's childhood torture, including being taken away from a child, assumed murdered at the age of two by her mother, who often took her to another town for unusual cult events. It was when Grace's life was in extreme turmoil that many other alters appeared.

According to Zoe, Grace went through many cycles in her life with DID, and often would win and lose friends. She finds it very hard to trust anyone, so Zoe plans on staying with Grace as long as she can to protect her.

Food, Alcohol, Weed, Pills —
Lots of Them — Acid and Jesus

Some of the addictions I've had while running away from my mind
I was always different. I was the fat, quiet girl with a life full of secrets.
Keeping all of them made me afraid of almost everyone. Doing everything, new or familiar, scared me so much. I was worried that people I
didn't know would talk to me and act like they knew me. Or, what if I
didn't know where I was? Sometimes people called me the wrong name.
I really hated wearing clothes I didn't remember putting on. If I got two
outfits, including socks and underwear, dirty, I was going to be in so much
trouble! I can never remember not worrying. It made my head hurt.

The first day of Kindergarten was the worst. I was so glad to be
sitting on the circle next to Timmy. He was my friend who lived
across the backyard from us. He never paid attention to my craziness.
Our mothers were right behind us. For me, that was terrible. I'd already been hit by the hairbrush all morning and yanked and pulled.
She asked me why I was so fat. Did I know how stupid I was? Mom
told me I wouldn't make any friends at school, and if I said one word

of our secrets I'd be on the big saw in the basement and sawed to pieces. Welcome to school…

While we were sitting in the circle, this loud girl kept running over to where Timmy and I were sitting. Her name was Sheila. She'd run over and look right at us and laugh and laugh. Her mom said "come here, honey," but she didn't stay. It was embarrassing! Finally, the nice teacher, Miss Robinson, thanked the nice mothers for coming and told them they could have us back after the morning class. The moms left. I think Timmy's and my mom got rides home from LaVonne, Debby's mom. Our moms didn't drive. Timmy and I were taking the bus home.

That was kind of the beginning of pretending to be okay in front of other people. There was church on Sunday mornings and evenings plus Wednesday nights, but I knew something more was wrong with me there. One day, in Sunday school, Mrs. Marquette was talking about Adam, Eve, the tree of knowledge and good and evil and the serpent. I raised my hand in front of everyone, and asked the teacher why Eve didn't think it was scary that the serpent talked to her. All of the kids laughed at me, but Mrs. Marquette was very angry! She said we'd meet with my parents after church to discuss the matter. When she told them what I said, my mom got tears in her eyes and my dad asked what the teacher thought. Perhaps Mack, her husband, should come in to discuss. I was so afraid. In my head I was saying: "I am, I am. I am." I said that when I was really, really scared. The people at church were important. I couldn't understand what they said. Then we were home and I was in my room without Sunday dinner until Sunday night and evening church, but all I remember was being at school on Wednesday.

A long time later I was told that the decision was that I wasn't pre-destined to be a Christian. In other words, these literal, arrogant ass-holes decided that no matter what I did, ever, I'll never get to heaven because God had already decided. Yay, Jesus!

The best thing about that church was the communion wine. They kept big bottles of yummy, Concord grape Mogen David in a cupboard by the back door. One of the bad boys, Mark, showed me at age 9. He was 8. We had a job. We emptied the communion goblet every Sunday, washed it and put it away. We split the rest of what was in the goblet, got two cloths (one wet and one dry) and carried the goblet to the cupboard where we filled it up and split it again. We washed out the goblet and put it away.

When I was about 12 years old I played a little piano. I liked to practice on the church's piano and drink some wine. It made me feel good. My back door key worked even after my family left that church. I used it until they sold the building when I was in 9th grade. I think I drank a lot of Mogen David. It made home a better place. It made confusion, fear and everything better. After that there was Strawberry Hill, Boone's Farm and wonderful people. There was always someone going to the store who would take my money and bring me a bottle.

But then I got confused and ended up in Charleston, Illinois. Across the Mississippi River was Charleston, Missouri. I didn't know how I'd gotten there, when, who with – no memory. But, there were wine bottles, beer bottles, Jim Beam bottles all over the room. I was in a motel. I waited for a day and night, but no one came. The next day my dad came. I know I was punished there and at home, but I don't remember any of it. A couple of my alters do, but this is about addiction.

I ate my way through school. I managed to be absent from school from 3rd grade until 6th grade on "weight day." My 6th grade teacher let me record weight and did mine last when no one was there. I weighed 160 pounds and she gave me a long, long lecture about the same old thing: "You're fat" and my head added "ugly and stupid and no one will ever care about you." My 2nd grade teacher put all of our weights on the board. I weighed 80 pounds in 2nd grade, two pounds more than the largest of the boys. I still hate that teacher, Mrs. Johnson, with her stupid smocks over her dresses every day. Her bully son was on crutches and got away with torturing anyone. Peer students made fun of me until the 8th grade all because of her. What a bitch!

In junior high school I found my mom's pills: blue ones were Valium, green and dark green capsules were Librium, grey and pink were Darvocet, grey and red, a little stronger, were Darvon and little white diet pills. White, long tablets for stronger pain, were Vicodin. I had to try them out one or two at a time to see how they made me feel. Oops, I forgot about the little ones which were lower doses of Valium. Mom kept medicine everywhere: in the cupboard with the dishes, on the side of the first shelf, and a lot more on the sides and in fancy containers with lids on the top shelf, the medicine cabinet, her underwear drawer and in my dad's hankie drawer. I wasn't snooping, but I was the one who had to clean out the cupboards and the medicine cabinet and put away laundry. I also ironed and folded dad's handkerchiefs and so much more.

A little experimenting and I didn't worry all of the time. Red and grey, pink and grey and yellow valium could block the pain of slaps a little more, saved me from Saturday nights. White ones, and I could clean everything and be pleasant. My mom liked me then. She'd call me "Callie" and laugh and be nice. We'd get popcorn at the Grant's store downtown, or hot cashews, peanut butter candies and safety pops when I was Callie – until she'd get tired of me.

One blue pill and I could sleep and sleep and sleep, but it didn't help me forget. So I ate, too. Then I found weed. What a great find. It's still my favorite, almost. I loved all kinds of acid, especially windowpane.

But, once the effects were gone, all of the bad stuff came back. Worry and fear along with always being confused were my feelings. Being called fat, stupid, ugly and unloved still resounds in my head.

Even though I earned really good grades, had a few good, good friends, and people would say "oh, that looks so pretty" or "you could be on a wedding cake, etc…" I never felt it then, nor do I now. Unfortunately, drugs of any kind do not last.

I tried Jesus now and then, but He always washed out. If they spoke in tongues, I had to check so that I'd speak in tongues. No one, ever, at any church said I was making it up. If they interpreted tongues, I'd stand up with a memorized message. No one ever pointed at me and said: "She's lying!" But I was. So much for Jesus. But, just like food, alcohol, weed, pills and acid, I often couldn't pass up a try at Jesus. Finally, I got my fill of Him when he hurt my son. But, drugs stay a small part of me, as does alcohol. And I'll never pass up a hit, a stamp or a mushroom, and I'm comfortable with my very own spirituality that doesn't fit in anyone else's place, because it's mine. It all helps me with the mental illness that will never go away.

Almost every morning I think I've gained one hundred pounds. I am too stupid to e-mail, and often decide that no one loves me. Fortunately, I have a therapist to point things out or to tweak my medicines. I still wear the same clothes I wore before I lost 100 pounds, but, yeah, like that will be true tomorrow?

I guess I'll add honey whiskey to my little bit of soda and a lot of ice, and hope my weedy friend comes by tomorrow. Sometimes I believe that I'm not crazy, just underappreciated and living here in the wrong dimension. Not a bad thing, just inconvenient.

Peace.

CARL

I was married to a veteran. He joined the army at 17 years of age and went to Korea. I believe he was there for three years. He became a career soldier and spent two tours of active duty as a combat soldier in Vietnam. Because of injuries he wasn't allowed to go back to combat, but finished his 20 years in Japan and Germany.

Carl was out of the military before PTSD was really recognized in the 1970s. And, knowing Carl, he would never discuss symptoms with a doctor. Instead, he drank. One of the things he first told me about Vietnam is that you were either a boozer or a druggie, both of which were readily available to the troops. Since he'd been drinking since the age of 14, he was a "boozer," or high-functioning alcoholic.

Carl was a Staff Sergeant; leading platoons through the jungle, teaching new soldiers and even new lieutenants. Apparently, freshly shipped lieutenants knew nothing about walking in a crouched position even when they were in the compound. A compound was an era stretched with concertina wire and had guards. Concertina wire is barbed wire with razors on the top.

When we first met, and during our first couple of years together, Carl didn't tell me much about his time in combat. He spoke of the severe weather: either freezing or intense heat. He said that there was a terrible smell in Korea. He thought it was all of the Kimchi buried everywhere. It is a cabbage preparation that is put in clay pots and buried underground until fermented. Carl thought of it as completely rotted and probably filled with rats that crawled in the pots. This is totally unconfirmed and seems unlikely. He also thought that the Koreans themselves smelled of Kimchi.

He was highly decorated in Vietnam. I'm thinking that I wasn't aware of this until we'd been married about four years, together six. He had two bronze stars, one with a V meaning he did something to risk his life and to save others. He had three silver stars, w of them with Vs, and a congressional medal of honor that he received after Vietnam and didn't go get. I asked him why. When he left his last military post, he dropped his duffel in his parents' barn and never opened it again.

Carl had violent dreams. I learned to sleep on the couch. He'd be aggressive if he awoke, yelling and ready to fight, yelling "DD Mou," meaning "move, move, hurry." I asked him after the first time. He used to tell me he didn't remember his dreams, but finally he began to share one of them with me. I bugged him about it because he'd yell in Vietnamese and curse in English, jump out of bed screaming "D D Mou" over and over. He would run out of the room and yell to people in his dreams to get down and stay. Then he'd just crumble to the ground. He'd done this several times saying he didn't know. Finally one night, when he was really drunk, he told me. The Vietnamese often booby-trapped their children. The GIs were used to giving candy or change to the local children.

Carl's dream was about a girl coming towards the concertina wire with a shoeshine box. He was responsible for his platoon when the lieutenant wasn't available. By the way the girl was walking, he felt she was booby-trapped, but couldn't be positive. Knowing Carl, I believe he would have never fired if he'd been alone, but he fired and the poor little girl blew up because, for whatever reasons, her parents let her be booby-trapped. The area they were in was controlled by South Korea and the United States. Chances were that she was a local child with a shoeshine box.

When we lived in California, we'd go to a VA hospital in Loma Linda. Even if I had to drive over 30 miles on the freeway in a thunderstorm while he was having a heart attack. While we were there and he had appointments, I found out about seminars and would go to them. When I told him about PTSD he denied having it and said it sounded like a catch-all for sissies. He felt the same way about me seeing a psychiatrist.

Carl's eldest son from his first marriage was immersed in stories about Vietnam. His mom and dad were divorced because he'd signed up for another tour of duty there. He and his dad had been apart for many years, so he was curious. Every time they talked about it for hours and hours, usually both of them drinking. It turned into a PTSD situation for Carl. Believing the "macho man" image of this father, the son would not listen to me.

I cannot remember which of the movies he brought for Carl and him to watch about Vietnam. I believe it was in the mid to late 80s when it was in the theatres. He brought it to watch when we were living in Mexico. They watched it the night before he and his family were leaving from their vacation with us.

His wife and kids and I went to town to shop and eat shrimp tacos on the beach. When we got home they were gone. No note, naturally. They got home near morning, and after good-byes my daughter-in-law drove off.

Carl went to bed and I went back to bed. I'd barely fallen asleep when I was being attacked. One thing I knew about Vietnam was that you couldn't always tell the difference between the enemy and farmers because they often wore what the Americans called pajamas. As he was beating me I understood "pajama fucking sneak." I was screaming at the top of my lungs to try and wake him up or come out of the episode he was in. I was finally able to grab a vase and crash it on his head, run away and get out of the house.

I ended up one street over and at the doctor's office. I needed a couple of stitches in my head and a butterfly bandage on my chin. I received a valium to calm my nerves (don't say "ah hah!"). It wasn't a very long time until I was divorced from the man who went on to wife #5, still saying that he didn't have a wussy disease called PTSD.

Living with an Addict

My second husband, Manuel Jimenez, was a heroin addict. I didn't re-alize this for the first thirteen months or so. I knew him while I was still living in San Felipe, Mexico. For the first two-and-a-half months, we talked and wrote while I was in Hunting Beach, California and he was in Mexicali, Mexico. We were married in December after he'd been in the United States with me for a month and one-half. We were in the states for eight months, went back to Mexico and I had our baby a week later. When he was about three months old I found his dad with a spoon and a syringe. When our son was two years old, he found him with a needle in his neck, believing he was dead. What a traumatic experience for a two-year-old.

We spent the next four years occasionally separating for him to go to rehab because he didn't want me alone in Mexico while he was away from home. Then he'd want us to come back because he couldn't make it through rehab without us. Once his mom and I got him through detoxing without professional help. Another time I did it on my own, but the longest he was ever clean was eight months. I remember him waking me up many times because he said heroin was calling him and we'd stay up all night talking through it. But the story behind his addiction is even more heartbreaking.

Meño's (his nickname) mom, Maria, was sold into a marriage by her father at the age of 13. The man was about 20 years her senior. He used Maria like a donkey with a harness and yoke across her shoulders to plow his fields. She had three children with him. He chased women and drank while she worked the fields. Plowing, planting and harvesting, she carried babies strapped to her back and front.

Maria would go to the house to cook, clean and wash clothes on a cement hand-made scrub board with water she'd carried from a stream about half a mile away. Many, many times she found her husband in their bed with another woman. He told her that this was normal and right. He was the man and she was his wife who he owned and she was to serve him and obey him. She even served the woman food if her husband told her to do it. She would leave less food for herself because she would never give her children less. Maria ate raw potatoes in the field. The potatoes were far away from the house, unlike the garden vegetables. He wouldn't walk out far enough to catch her eating. The children thought they were treats and knew not to tell "Poppy."

By the time she was 18, Maria had her third child, and was exhausted, depressed and had no hope for a better future. Worse yet, she had no hope for her children's futures. Going "home" was not an option, as her father would have beaten her and then taken her back to the man he sold her to. Her mother and sisters would have been powerless to help her. So, she took off with her children one night when she knew her husband would be gone for at least three days.

They wore all of the clothes they had, which was probably no more than three outfits each. She'd sew them by hand. Maria was a great seamstress. Later in life she could look at a photo of any outfit, gown, pants or shirt in a magazine and recreate it exactly, stitching all by hand.

Maria and her children travelled to a village on the border near Arizona, quite far from the farmland. Mexico has its own traditions and ways of life. By jumping over a broom three times, Maria was a divorced woman. She met and married her second husband when the baby turned a year old. My husband, Meño was her second in this marriage. She had two boys. Meño's older brother took after their father's Spanish side of the family and has red hair and blue eyes. Bu Meño has his name, Jesus Manuel Moreno-Condi. Condi was his mother's maiden name. He ended up using his step-father's last name of Jimenez instead of Moreno.

The family moved to Mexicali, Mexico on the Baja California. Mexicali is the capital of Baja California, and a very large city with a population of close to 700,000. Once they were there and somewhat settled, Manuel Moreno just disappeared. Maria never knew if it was another woman or if he had somehow been killed. She began drinking heavily at this time. Then she met her third husband, Pedro, a wonderful man from a nearby tienda de abboretos, a grocery store. He started dropping off groceries to them when he learned of their circumstances.

Pedro started going around looking for Maria and convinced her to stop drinking and marry him. She told me that she truly loved this husband. She had four children with him: a girl, two boys, and another girl. The older children had moved on by now. Unfortunately, when the last two children were a year old and an infant, Pedro was diagnosed with cancer and died nine months later.

There are no widow's benefits, social security or welfare in Mexico. Maria had reconnected with two of her older brothers after moving to Mexicali. They lived on ranches, one a bit to the southeast, up in the mountains. They weren't usual ranches, as their primary crop was marijuana. They wouldn't just give their sister money to live on. Instead, they gave her pounds of marijuana to sell, 10 pounds a month with her share being $20.00. I believe it was in 1978. Her brothers could make as much as $1,500. Maria, of course, had no idea. Twenty dollars was about 32 pesos, enough to exist on.

Meño was nine, and his brother Germán was ten. They were the ones selling at that time. Maria had babies to care for. She was able to obtain land in the form of homesteading on the outskirts of Mexicali at a place named El Jido. Sometimes she and the older boys had to defend their property with a rifle. Today, there is a house with built-on rooms. It is now in the city. In 2004 they were going to pave the road in front.

Maria had an older daughter in San Felipe, Mexico. She was married and she and her husband had jobs and children. Meño took 5 pounds of weed to San Felipe, a 126 mile trek to the coast of the Sea of Cortez. It was 1982. Americans were coming to the area for the beach, the seafood, the experience. The fishing village was growing. Meño met up with some Americans who gave him $100 for his 5 pounds. He took his mom $70 and then went back to San Felipe.

Unfortunately, both of the boys started to smoke what they were selling, but managed to keep even with what the uncles took in their cut. Maria never had a chance to learn to read or count, so she didn't know how much her brothers were cheating her. The uncles didn't know how much American tourists were paying the boys. Everyone was happy.

The uncles then gave the family cocaine and heroin to sell. Germán liked the cocaine. Meño liked the heroin. Pretty soon their world fell apart. They used more than they sold, especially Meño. At the age of 15, he had to run because his uncles were now part of a large drug cartel and hit men were sent out to kill him. It made no difference that he was family or that he was so young.

Meño had become resourceful before forced to run. His half-sister had kicked him out because of his drug use, so he lived on the beach. He begged from tourists and dug clams, caught fish and knew fishermen willing to trade drugs for fish until they had the drugs and Meño then helped himself. So, he really, really had to get far away.

He made his way to the southern tip of Baja. Even there he spotted one of the hit men. A local fisherman took him out to an island.

There was a lot of wind, colder weather and more rain than Meño had ever known, but he was safe. I can't imagine how awful detoxing all alone on an island must have been. When he told me about this he said he felt like he hallucinated for years, was sick and always cold and hungry. There were bananas or plantains most likely, and he dug clams and caught fish, eating them raw. It was three years until he went back to his mother's in Mexicali.

Unfortunately, three of his older brothers were around, also heroin addicts. His younger brother was an alcoholic, and so was Maria. She could, and did, stay sober for months at a time, but then she'd slide back. Most of her daughters worked, at least part-time, as hookers. They'd married alcoholics and had to feed their babies.

When I knew Maria, only her daughter, in San Felipe, was clean, sober and employed, as was the man she married. I know Maria drank to relieve the guilt she felt. I tried to convince her that she did the best she could, that her grown children made their choices, and that poverty had led her into slavery and later paid for her freedom and a house of her own.

The trauma of the life they led was full of mental illness and torment. Meño's younger brother drank, running from schizophrenia. Before Germán died from suicide, he was a narcissist who believed he was invincible and better than everyone. Meño became paranoid over time, and couldn't control his anger. He had PTSD from the threat on his life, and probably a few more issues added in. He taught his younger brother how to shoot up. Maria told me they shot up after being clean for close to a year, then died together.

Our son was fourteen. We didn't hear about his father's death until he was sixteen. It had been thirteen years since he'd heard from or seen Meño. He has struggled with pain and genetics, always, bust most of the struggle is over. He is strong, productive, intelligent and wonderful. The sadness I have for his father is that he never knew this amazing young man.

Overused and Meaningless

Anne and Her Childhood

We begin this story about someone with depression and suicidal tendencies. This person suffered from abuse at an early age and would often withdraw to her room or the backyard to avoid confrontation. We shall name her Anne. Books were her best friends as she could read at a fourth grade level at the age of three. And why shouldn't they be? After all, she would find herself identifying with her fictional companions rather than subject herself to the realities of life. Did this help to learn to cope with issues? DEFINITELY NOT!

Growing up in a strict Catholic family, Anne was often confused by the teachings of the church versus the realities of life. Her father was an abusive man who suffered from alcoholism. Her mother, Mary, was open-minded, yet was an enabler for her father William, believing that if she did what the father desired that all would be well in the family. The sad part is, rather than communicating, they lived in fear of consequences that would occur if they did not comply with the father's wishes.

Besides her parents, she had one older sister, Bonnie, who was also very abusive. She would beat on Anne mercilessly. Because Bonnie was much stronger, Anne's only form of self-defense was biting or scratching since she had long nails and her sister bit hers down to the quick. Anne was reprimanded for scratching her older sister, as the scratch marks were obvious. Another tell-tale sign left behind that blamed Anne for being the abuser rather than defending herself were the teeth marks she would leave in Bonnie's arms while being attacked. There was no denying the owner of the teeth marks, as Anne had bucked teeth that protruded in the shape of a "V." Bonnie would run to her parents to cry about the bite marks.

However, the bruises that Anne obtained from her sister's beatings would not manifest themselves until several days after a big fight. Her mother, Mary, actually took Anne to the doctor because she was concerned that she was bruising too easily. The doctor recommended taking additional Vitamin C. No one ever asked if there had been any type of physical altercation.

Needless to say, Anne was named the evil sister, while Bonnie was commended for her virtuous ways, even though she would often do "little" things like cutting the hair off of Anne's dolls or cutting Anne's fingernails so short that they would bleed. To be fair, Bonnie was the more quiet of the two, and Anne was often called rambunctious. To cover up her mean streaks, Bonnie would turn around and do something nice to try to amend for her wrongful acts. She would make or buy clothes for Anne's dolls, or bring her presents, thereby appearing to be the "nice" one.

Their father, William, found love in his work. He would much rather spend time at the shop than spend time with his family. Only attending school until the 10th grade, after his two years in the army he worked at the same factory until his death which was caused from radiation poisoning during his time spent in Japan during WWII. He arrived in Japan 3 days after the bombs were dropped. Some of his issues may have been from the slowly developing cancer in his blood that settled in his brain and lungs. There were very few cases of this type of cancer, and 95% of the affected were Japanese citizens. Was he ever given help from the VA? No, because what happened to his life during wartime was owned by the government. There were no treatments for PTSD during World War II, or so Anne was told, even though there was discussion of shell shock, but not in his case. If he would have been poisoned during testing of the bombs they would have helped him, but since he was serving in the Army during the war, at that time, he was given no help. Drinking a fifth of liquor each night when he came home along with a few beers was his "treatment." Sundays were martini days. Gin was not his friend, and he became a violent man on those days.

So William worked for the same company upon returning from the war, and moved up in a factory of 3,000 employees to the rank of upper management. His next promotion would have been that of Vice-president of the company, as he was a very intelligent man despite his lack of a high school diploma.

Anne's mother was very naïve when she met my father. She did not even learn about sex until the night before her wedding when her mother gave her "the talk." Mary seriously considered calling off the marriage. Mary lived in her fairy tale world, believing in prince charming, even though her formative years happened during a disastrous family life. Her father was a philanderer who called his wife a skinny bitch, supposedly molesting Mary's older sister Betty as well as his sister-in-law Elinore among others, and he often was gone for three or more days at a time while he was drunk and sleeping with other women. Mary's mother, Lucille, stayed with him for two reasons only: their two children and he was good in bed. When the girls were old enough to get married, Anne's grandparents divorced.

Mary's older sister became pregnant after dropping out of school at a relatively young age. She was living with her boyfriend and future husband with Mary's family (still together at that time). A lot of people never knew that Betty was pregnant when she married, as she had a miscarriage shortly after the wedding. Most of Mary's friends "had" to get married, but Mary was oblivious to sex and the jokes and stories her friends would tell. Mary married William because he was a good Catholic boy who would never cheat on his wife, was a good provider, and was a good-looking 6'2 blond. Mary was very lovely as well, and did quite a bit of modeling, so she had no problem finding the man of her dreams. She converted to Catholicism and followed all of the rules even if she didn't agree with them. Mary had actually been baptized in the Catholic religion, but her parents never practiced it so she had to go through the conversion process.

There were many arguments in Anne's household as a child. William was lord and master of the home. He called everyone fat, lazy and stupid. He ordered the family to do most of the chores in the household, including sorting out his wood after he was finished with yet another project. It should be mentioned that Anne was number one in her class until the final quarter of her senior year in high school, as she was told that she must be valedictorian, yet had no professional speaking skills. She would freeze in giving oral reports in school to her friendly classmates. She pleaded that she would embarrass the school if she were to give a speech. Finally, by not turning in homework and intentionally doing poorly the final quarter of the year, she managed to bring herself down to number four in the class rankings. Whew! What a relief! No need to give a speech.

Yes, William called them all lazy. Perhaps it was because they were never given the opportunity to explore their personal interests. They were not allowed to spend the night at friends' houses, nor were they allowed to participate in any activities away from school or home. William was in command of the whereabouts of his family at all times, and home was his answer. As soon as Bonnie and Anne were 11, they were babysitting, and by the time they were 16, it was demanded that the children had weekend and evening jobs. Heck, even at the ages of eight and four, Bonnie and Anne were out hawking vegetables from the garden which they tended all during the summer.

And yes, the children were chubby. This was amazing since William was 6'2" and 135 pounds and Mary was 5'8" weighing in at a lowly 115 pounds. They had to eat everything loaded on their plates and could not drink anything until the meal was over. It was nutritious food, and very rarely had sweets or even desserts, but were ordered to eat large portions of everything on the plate as William had grown up in a large Catholic family during the depression where good food was a priceless commodity. Besides that, children were starving in China!

So, by now you have a pretty good picture of Anne's childhood home life. So far it doesn't sound too bad. There are many who have suffered much worse. We won't even mention the spankings or standing in the corner for hours on end for "misbehaving." That was the common practice of parenting during the baby boomer years. There was the time that Anne was walking home from school the day before Thanksgiving, and another student was driving his car, came up over the curb and hit Anne, throwing her 50' into the air, nearly ripping off her entire ear upon landing on her head, but was fortunate to survive with extreme bruising due to the snow and the large fluffy bear coat that was so popular. Even though put on trial medicines to control the bruising and the use of a type of super glue to hold her ear in place, her dad insisted that she attend the family Thanksgiving fest, which was commanded by his family. They went to church in the morning, followed by a feast of wonderful food as well as drunken relatives. They stayed until 2 am because the "boys" liked to play poker all night. No thought was given to the extreme pain Anne was enduring.

Perhaps William beating up Anne and her mother might have been a bit over the top when Anne asked her dad to help her sell the last five candy bars for school. He was always bringing candy home that he purchased from others at work. Anne escaped the house when he started beating on her mother because she was trying to protect Anne, but William followed after her with the car nearly running her down while all of the neighbors were watching. No one would help Anne. It was none of their business. Anne's idea of escaping was hiding in her room or on the dark side of the house to read or cry. Bonnie would stay in her room and crank up hard rock and roll music before it was even popular! Of course, she would place the record player along the wall that connected their rooms, so if Anne stayed in her room when Bonnie was home, she could not find solitude inside the house. Thus, her retreat to the outside of her home where the sun never shone.

At this time it must be mentioned that Anne's father and sister were both left-handed. Of course, the nuns beat William into writing with his right hand because the alternative was a sign of the devil. Although that sounds "mystical," it has been noted that those who are left-handed have a higher rate of schizophrenic or sociopathic/bi-polar behavior. Anne's now adult left-handed daughter is also an example of this theory as well, sweet many times, but very unstable with many relationships.

The Teen Years and Early Adulthood

To tell the truth, Anne struggled with her weight all of her life. She was put on a diet of 2% milk when she was only six weeks of age. Protruding teeth did not enhance her beauty. Her father did not want her to get her eyes tested because he thought she was doing it because everyone else was getting glasses. He never apologized when finding out she was nearly blind and ended up wearing very thick lenses. She starved herself to be of relatively normal weight, and braces and contacts (Anne had to pay for those herself) greatly improved her appearance. So much so that she won the local Miss American Teenager contest of a very large county.

As mentioned before, Mary had been a model for several years. To her, life was all about beauty. When going on the typical long Sunday drives in cars without air conditioning, they were never allowed to open the windows because it would "muss up" their hair. Needless to say, it certainly did not help Anne's motion sickness attacks for which she was chastised. Before school, while everyone else was sleeping, Anne had to get up at 4:00 a.m. to wash and set her hair and sit under a professional hair dryer while everyone else was sleeping. She was "blessed" with stick-straight and oily hair, so it was a daily ritual.

High school years were relatively normal. Anne dated quite a bit, despite her nerdiness of being number one in the class. Although, her father only allowed dates to be on Tuesday nights between 6 and 9 and on Saturday nights from 6 to midnight (curfew for the town) or earlier. Most of the time those dates did not go well, ending up with only one date. One of her dates wouldn't walk her to the door because it was raining outside. She just hadn't learned to cope with those who were different from her upbringing. That probably happens to most of us in the early dating years, especially to those who were over-protected.

Anne finally met a boy who did not go to her school. He was a cousin of one of her best friends, and he lived in a nearby town. He was so in love with her that as soon as Anne's sister got married, he proposed to Anne although she was only sixteen and he was barely eighteen. She thought about it for a while, but realized she needed to feel more for someone that she married. There was no spark, even though he was a great kisser and looked like Brad Pitt. He just was not "the one" after two years of dating. She was still a virgin. A few more one-night dates happened before she found the man of her dreams, Dave. He made her laugh, he made her feel special when he wasn't out with the guys playing tennis or poker, he made love to her so tenderly, for hours on end. He was the perfect man: smart, Catholic, in college, good looking. Need we say more? He was her one and only lover, or so she thought. They were engaged at the ripe old age of 19.

They had made a lot of future plans. He was to go to college and Anne was to stay at home and work full-time to save up for their marriage after he received his Bachelor degree. Then, she would be able to go to college full-time and he could work full-time while working on his Masters Degree. Life was remarkable. He never informed her that he was also planning on earning his Doctorate. More about that later.

In his junior year of college, Dave explained that he had a part time job taking out a girl whose father gave him $50 a week to make sure she would mingle with the right type of people. Anne was informed that this "Sally" was the slut of the campus and Dave had absolutely no interest in her at all. Many years later, after Dave's divorce, Anne found out that Sally was actually the respectable head cheerleader at his college and definitely did not have a problem connecting with people of influence. Yet another lie revealed. When the winter dance came around that year, Anne bought herself the most expensive and flattering dress she could find, hoping she would run into this poor "Miss Sally," to show her she was his fiancé and that she shouldn't even try to go near him romantically. They had just become engaged, and Anne wanted Sally to see the very large and beautiful ring. As far as Anne knew, they did not run into each other at the dance. Dave probably told her not to attend.

By June of that same year, Anne had caught him in so many lies that she took her saved money and bought a brand new Mustang. She drove the car well over 100 mph on the Wisconsin back roads, hoping to drive off of the road. When totally lost, she slowly retraced her route back to northern Illinois, hitting her beautiful engagement ring against the doorframe the whole time. When she returned to town, she went to Dave and threw the ring back at him. A week later he was in a terrible bike accident and needed plastic surgery. Of course, she really did still love him. Anne went up to his hospital room while his sister was keeping Sally from going up the elevator. More will be discussed later, but years afterwards Dave told Anne he never met Sally until after they had broken up. He couldn't remember his own lies! Yet, Anne was the type of person who would consider hurting someone's feelings if she had to tell them the truth. That was of utmost importance to her.

So, they went their separate ways. Anne moved away from home with her friend and became a short-lived hippy. Yes, she tried pot, acid, crystal meth, mushrooms, but not heroin because too many of her friends knew people who had died from overdoses. She dated several men at a time. She could not deal with such an unstructured and uncertain future. She continued to work full-time, and started attending college part time. Dave called her up at work only a few months after his ring was returned to tell her that he and Sally were engaged. Why would he want to marry the campus slut? He wanted Anne to hear it from him first. She was devastated. How could he tell her news like that while she was at work?

The night before he got married he called Anne up to tell her that he loved only Anne and was only marrying Sally because he didn't want to hurt her like he did Anne. When he received his PhD, he called her up to tell her how petrified he was that he'd now have to find a real job. He and Sally were married and living in Ames, Iowa at the time. How dare he complain about finding a job when Anne had only started working full-time at a bank in order to save for their future rather than immediately attend college.

Before he moved out east with his terrific wife Sally, he called Anne and asked to meet with her to talk. By this time, Anne was living with a wonderful man, Tom, who treated her like a queen, but did not believe in marriage. They had a 2-year-old at the time. Anne's mother watched her son and told her mother that she was meeting with Dave to talk to get everything out of their system, and that she was taking a pizza to his hotel so they could eat while they talked. Mary knew that Anne had never stopped loving Dave. First loves are hard to forget.

As soon as Anne got to the room, her heart melted. Yes, she still loved the man, and was hoping he was going to tell her he was leaving his wife. He started getting frisky. When she asked Dave his intentions he said he hoped they could meet once a year or so for a sexual rendezvous. Well, Anne stormed out of the room, hurt and unfulfilled. There was no affair as he had wished. She did not hear from him again for a long time. Many years later Anne was told by Dave's sister that his marriage to Sally was sexless.

Anne had interrupted her college studies while raising two children. She let them engage in all of the activities they wanted, whether affordable or not. They had a Montessori education. There was dance, poms, track, figure skating, theatre and more. They were allowed to attend almost any event, even though they were requested to work to help pay for some of their activities. They were far from wealthy. One might even say Tom and Anne were on the poor end of the scale. Anne returned to full-time work while the children were still young, and returned to finish her college education on a part-time basis (still working full-time) when the children were old enough to be by themselves for a few hours a few nights a week.

Anne was determined to earn her degree that was passed up by falling in love. She never blamed anyone for that except herself, because that was her decision. She could have gone to college right after high school with a full-paid scholarship, but Anne was in "love" and her parents really didn't care whether or not she continued on with her education. Going to college for girls was only an excuse to find a husband. Bonnie found her husband in her sophomore year in college, where she basically majored in pinochle and partying. That marriage lasted about nine years, with one son for Bonnie to raise on her own. Anne finally received her degree, summa cum laude, two months before her oldest child earned his college degree.

In her heart, she still yearned for Dave. She had not had sex with her partner for many years, and so longed for the passion she once had. However, Anne lived a relatively happy life without him, as she kept busy with work, school, kids, theatre, and had a wonderful man supporting her emotionally the entire time. After over 40 years, they are still together and unmarried. She always told her children that if they could not end up with the perfect person, to "settle" for a person who loved you more than you loved them. In retrospect, she feels this was not necessarily good advice.

During those years, technology had advanced tremendously. Anne was taking a few college and continuing education courses online.

While searching for articles for her thesis, she ran across a picture of Dave with his work cronies winning an amateur tennis event. She does not deny that she had searched for him (and other old friends) online in the past, only to find nothing prior to this accidental story, so she gave up wasting her time and figured that he just hadn't done anything noteworthy nor was on any social media. Most everyone searches for past friends on the Internet, thus the success of Facebook and other social media past and present. Searching is not just for stalkers. Anyhow, when clicking on the picture it told the story of the team, their work address and e-mail addresses. Anne e-mailed him and asked if he was the same Dave from their Northern Illinois High School. He replied yes, and figured that it must have been a coincidence that she ran across his picture as he had just been thinking of her because they were nearing that 50-year-old age mark, and was probably a mid-life memory check.

A few years later Anne was working on a time-limited grant, and Tom had lost his job due to the poor economy (especially in a blue collar manufacturing town). The outlook of finding a job in their town was dismal to say the least. Tom was offered a job in South Carolina and she recommended that he take it. They had thought about retiring there and it just seemed the right thing to do. Since Anne knew her job would be ending soon, it appeared to be the most intelligent choice. Their daughter wasn't certain about continuing her education, so she moved south as well. They lived by the beach and were and are very happy. Anne hadn't heard from Dave for quite a while, so life was good in the new surroundings. They bought a house exactly one mile away from the beach so they could walk there whenever they wanted, yet wouldn't have to worry too much about hurricane issues. She found a job right away, and then was offered a much better job less than one year later. However, the grass isn't always greener. For the most part, working in South Carolina in the beach region is like being in prison or a slave. Bosses do not care about labor laws and will treat their employees like chattel. It was quite a culture shock. She only held that job for a few years.

Several years passed and their daughter moved back up to Illinois to complete her college education. Their son never moved down with them because he was establishing his career in the Chicago area and had a child to care for.

The Fiasco

All hell broke loose and Tom was diagnosed with severe bladder cancer and massive prostate cancer. He spent the better part of six months off of work between the several surgeries and complications. They used up most of his retirement. Returning to work, he was still in severe pain and taking several pain medications, but fortunately the cancer was gone. And that was all that mattered to them, even though Anne was currently working a low-paying retail job due to the economy.

Ah, yes, there are always caveats, the yin and yang, the karma. Tom was cured, but depressed. He began drinking heavily while taking too many pain medications. He was not the man he had always been. He was living in a stupor and Anne was very unhappy, even though she kept trying to cheer him up and support him. After several years, Anne told Tom that she would leave him if he didn't change back to his old self, or at least try.

Timing hit Anne's life once again. Dave e-mailed her to tell her his ex-wife and son had moved to Myrtle Beach, and would she be interested in meeting him for breakfast when he flew down to visit his son. She hesitated, as it had been about 25 years since seeing him, and they both had most certainly aged, yet she agreed to meet him for breakfast. That was when he told her he was remarried. She doubted very much if she would have met him knowing this, as she knew what he wanted years ago when taking him the pizza. She had hoped that he had matured since then, and she never desired to be the "other woman."

However, nothing happened, and they met for breakfast about once every 6 months when he would visit his grown son. One day when his son was working, Dave took Anne out on an all day tour event until it started raining. They were hoping the rain would stop so they could walk along the beach for a while, but the rain continued as their hormones kicked in while sitting in the car. After talking for quite a while, he asked her what she wanted. She told him that she wanted to be fondled. It had been close to 30 years since Tom and she had been intimate. Dave had no problem complying, but they limited themselves to kissing and a few touches on the breasts over the clothes.

The next time he came to the beach he asked Anne to join him in his room. She declined, as she knew she was weak. The following trip she did go up to his hotel room, but told him it was for coffee and talking only. They chatted quite a while on the balcony, but she had to leave in a hurry because Anne could not trust herself.

Later on that year, Anne went on a solo vacation to take some time away from Tom. He was still having drinking and drug problems, and they spent a lot of time just staying apart as much as possible, and Anne felt so helpless and unloved. It was the first time she had spent time away from him except to visit her mother in Illinois once or twice a year. She loved nature, and found a wildlife refuge in Maryland where they were saving whooping cranes. Finding out that Patuxent was not that far from where Dave was living and working, he decided that he would take a day off to visit Washington, DC and visit some museums, see the White House and take Anne to dinner and a play. It was during dinner that he told her that his first wife Sally had just lost a baby shortly before the time he met her for pizza in Illinois years ago.

He came to Anne's room in Patuxent after the play, and she was really hoping he would stay, but he went home to his wife. Mind you, he had told Anne very little about his second wife except that she was a little crazy, believing she is clairvoyant and is an empath. She had her own business, but he didn't know what it was, even though she ran it from home. He thought she had a college degree, but was not sure what it was. Her ex-husband was very rich. She had two children about the same age as his. They had not had sexual relations for a long time because she had interstitial cystitis and it was too painful for her. Of course she also had Lyme's complications, although Dave never said she was ever diagnosed with Lyme's. She had multiple imaginary illnesses Anne was told, although Dave did not seem to be aware that most of her diseases are not considered illnesses. There was no way to test for most of them. Dave told Anne that he would divorce Jann now, but didn't want to go through that horrible experience again. It sounded like his life was so loveless, and Anne wanted to give him everything.

The next time he came to South Carolina, he invited Anne to his hotel room. They started with coffee, as they had the time before, then started to discuss sex and how it wasn't anything they hadn't done before, and since he and she had sexless lives, that perhaps they could at least fulfill each other in that manner. Dave told her that he had never cheated on any of his women and that he wasn't going to start. Anne was perplexed since she knew he had been dating Sally while they were engaged, and that he tried to cheat with her while he was married to Sally, and that by going out with her he was basically cheating on his current wife, Jann. Anne had also been told by others in his family that he had cheated on his first wife Sally with Jann. Of course, there was also a rumor that he must have spread about Anne having affair with him while he was married to Sally because Sally's mom called up Dave's mom to yell at her about it. She told his mom to tell Dave to keep it in his pants. Where did Sally's mom get that information? Had Dave bragged to Sally that he had an affair? It never happened. Not with Anne, anyhow. Although he did tell many stories about close encounters while he was on the road for work. He did travel a lot to California, North Carolina and Taiwan for long periods of time as he created electronic computer parts for many globally-known companies.

Ultimately, in their fifties, they did have a real affair, still meeting only every six months or so, but they always made up for lost time sexually. He could still last all night and give Anne so many orgasms that he made her feel like she was physically and emotionally in ecstasy. Anne told him she still loved him and longed for him. His response was that the term love was "overused and meaningless." That response hurt Anne more than Dave would ever know. To be fair, however, Anne was stupid enough to fall for him again after being hurt so badly in her younger years.

But then came more lies and forgetfulness. He said he couldn't understand why Anne didn't go to college right away after high school. He didn't remember ever discussing the agreement they had made before they became engaged, the part about Anne working while he earned his degree, etc. They had both gone to the same highly-respected Catholic school, but had both become atheists over the years. He would even e-mail Anne comments he had replied to others about his atheism. Anne had started a Humanist group in Myrtle Beach shortly after moving there. Once again he denied that he ever met Sally until after they broke off their engagement. One of the stipulations of the affair was to notify either one of them if they had sex with anyone, including spouses/significant others. That agreement had made it seem like safe sex to Anne. He had a vasectomy (first he told Anne it was because Sally had a hard time carrying babies to term and he didn't want to go through that any more because they already had two children, yet another time he told her that Jann wanted more kids, so he had the vasectomy then, and that he had to have it done twice because the first time it didn't take and he still had active sperm).

He told Anne that he had custody of his two children from his first marriage because Sally was an unfit mother who had tried to kill herself by overdose. Anne found out later from his sister that he did not raise his children, but that they used his address so they could go to the better high school in town. When he divorced Sally, he paid for her Masters degree. When Dave and Jann got married, his son tried to kill himself by slashing himself up and down both arms. He would be dead if his new step-brother had not found him while Jann and Dave were on their honeymoon. Sally and her new husband and his son were still living in the same town when Dave got remarried. Dave told Anne that Sally was crazy and eventually had to get away from Maryland to avoid running into him.

Now comes the hard part. Dave ended up getting bladder cancer that had spread to his lymph nodes. Anne felt terrible about this as she had no way of contacting him concerning his health progress. Yes, Anne stupidly still loved him, but the last time she had met him was when he invited her to his home while Jann was out of town. Jann had left a "Honey Do" list on their counter. The "to do" list included "make whoopee" and Anne confronted him with that since he told her they weren't having sex due to her physical ailments. He then told Anne that once in a while she let him have sex if it wasn't too painful. This was the lie that truly ended the affair, even though Anne did meet with him a week before his surgery for a pity fuck because she knew it would probably be the last time he'd ever have great sex since they were going to remove his bladder and prostate and the nerves would be damaged.

The morning of Dave's surgery, Anne sent him a text wishing him well. He had been upset because his surgery was at 1:30 pm and he'd rather have the first of the day. So, while Anne was getting ready for work she sent a text message wishing they could share and make pleasant memories for him to think about while he was recovering. She was always careful not to send any suggestive messages.

His wife texted Anne back on his phone saying he was in surgery and AnnaMarie (that is what came up on his phone) could check on him later. Obviously, Anne was shocked. She never wanted his wife to find out. If he would have only told Anne that the surgery had been rescheduled.

Jann immediately told him that AnnaMarie had said she wanted to give him a little bit of heaven before his surgery, and later on he kept insisting that was the message that was sent, so Jann must have deleted the real message. As an atheist, those are words Anne would never write. Dave ended up having complications from his surgery as the cancer had spread to his lymph nodes. However, as far as Anne knew, he was cured, even though he had a urostomy due to the loss of his bladder. Even if Anne would have been hurt by the relatively innocent text, she would have never gone off on Dave the minute he got out of surgery. She would have waited until he felt well enough to have an honest discussion, something he doesn't seem to know much about.

About a week later Anne sent an email to his work address, knowing what a workaholic he was. She wanted to check to see how he was doing. He called when Jann was out of the hospital room to say he had complications and that he'd contact her when he was able because Jann was monitoring all of his calls, texts and emails.

Several days later Anne called his sister to see how he was doing, because he should have been out of the hospital, but his mother answered the phone. She told Anne to continue calling her to find out his status since Jann was not letting him talk to anyone. Jann did not get along with his family, Anne was told. His mom told her that he'd be in the hospital a while longer.

Anne called up the nurse's station not to find out his health condition, as there are HIPPAA rules, but to see if it would be safe to send him flowers. They said to go ahead and send them. They were sent with the initials of his pet name for her, with an "Inc" at the end. His wife tracked down the FTD florist it was sent from, even though the flowers were paid with cash and a real name was not left with the florist. Who knows? Maybe he used the same pet name for his wife? The flowers were sent on St. Patrick's Day, as Dave was Irish and was in the hospital on March 17. Jann probably shattered them. Anne might have done the same if it were her. She truly understood Jann's anger, as Anne had been cheated on with Dave in the past, and she knew how she felt at the time.

At the end of March, Anne called Dave's mom, Donna, again and she told Anne that Dave was now at home, but Jann wouldn't let him talk to anyone unless she initiated the call. His mother asked that Anne call her up to check on his condition. His sister then asked Anne not to talk to his mom again because it upset her, even though all conversations had been extremely pleasant. Remember, Anne was actually calling up Dave's sister, but his mother lived with her and mom answered the phone when she saw the name on caller ID. Anne complied. However, she did mail or call the Maryland police department to ask them to stop by Dave's house since it seemed that his wife was not sharing things with anyone, and that she had taken charge of all of his communication, including his work messages. She did not say that he was being abused, but that she was concerned and was hoping they would check to make sure he was ok. She never spoke to Dave's mom again. She would only email the sister from that time on. That only lasted a few months before things changed because Anne was accused of sending the police to the house due to spousal abuse. Another lie. Three years later, Dave's mom Donna died.

Anne then sent Dave an e-mail at his work asking if she could visit with his son, because he had always said they'd get along well because Anne would be able to help his son with his weight issues because he knew Anne was always struggling with hers. They also liked to read similar books. His son did live a relatively normal life until his suicide attempt when his father married Jann. In fact, he had been quite popular in his younger days, getting two girls pregnant so Dave had said. One child was adopted out Anne had been told during an earlier conversation during the Patuxent visit. The other was aborted, and Anne had only recently learned of that second pregnancy before Dave's surgery.

Dave never answered Anne's text, even though Dave had returned to work and was planning on renewing their vows at the beach in Mid-April. Why would he do that at the beach except to try to upset Anne and Sally? Ben would never attend his dad's vows, as he really was petrified of Jann. His son lived in his own condominium, worked and drove a great car and was in his 30s, even if he was on disability for psychological issues. Anne really didn't feel she needed permission to speak to him, as they were all adults, but out of respect for Dave and his family, she thought it was the proper thing to do. So, in April, after trying to commit suicide by overdose due to extreme bullying by Dave and his wife via e-mail and text, Anne left a note on Dave's son's car with her phone number stating she was an old friend of his father and that his dad had said it would be nice if they could meet since they had so much in common. Anne always walked on the beach the same time every day, so Anne told him when and where she parked when walking at the beach. Ben, Dave's son, never called Anne, so she was surprised when he did show up on a drizzly day in April. She never told him that she was his dad's lover, but he did know about her from stories his dad did tell him about her from years ago. Ben and Anne spoke of books and diets and depression only.

After the nice conversation, Dave called Anne and left a message that how dare she talk to his son. He told her that his son told him that they had talked about his ex-girlfriends and that she knew their names. They never talked about his girlfriends and Anne certainly didn't know their names. She didn't know where Dave got his information, but nothing was spoken about that was private except that yes, Anne was his dad's old fiancé, Anne, and that, yes, she still cared about him and was concerned about his surgery. Ben must remember how he felt about his first love and would be concerned if he knew that she was ill. And that was the only comment that was made about past love. Those words could have been mentioned to anyone. However, when Anne mentioned the name Jann, Ben started shaking and panicking. Dave had told Anne that he was staying with his ex-wife when he visited Ben, and Anne had mentioned how nice it was of his new wife to allow Dave to stay with her. Ben insisted this was not true and that Dave never stayed at Sally's house. Another lie. She was not surprised.

Of course, then Jan, Jann, Janna (depending on her mood) continued sending Anne threatening texts and e-mails. Dave told Anne it was because Jann was drinking heavily and she didn't mean it. She threatened to come down to Myrtle Beach at Tom's work and tell him everything because she owned her own business and had the flexibility to come and go as she pleased. His sister started to send Anne mean e-mails saying that Dave had taken karate and could take care of Tom. Anne simply wrote back to her saying that Tom would never beat anyone up, but that he could certainly handle himself if Dave tried anything, as Tom had taken Shotokan Japanese karate as well as being 100 lbs. larger than Dave. He could certainly defend himself if he ever encountered a confrontation. Being a pacifist, Anne would have never considered a physical altercation, yet Anne was accused of saying that she was going to send Tom to beat up Dave. That was never an option, nor was ever said.

Then Jann emailed an artificial restraining order with threats attached, letting Anne know how stupid she was. Anne replied to the e-mail that if she were so smart she would know that a restraining order with a threat or blackmail attached is meaningless. Jann continued to send threats and restraining order comments, accusing Anne of sending them things that she never did. Anne had to get Amazon Prime to contact them to tell them to stop harassing Anne for something she never did. Of course, Amazon could not tell Anne who sent those books about paleo diets and philosophy, but Jann "knew" they were from her since Anne was an atheist and would be the type of person to send those things. Jann also kept insisting that Anne had sent the text wishing she could give Dave a little bit of heaven. So, why would she think an atheist would write those words?

Anne did admit the things she had done: sent flowers to Dave at the hospital, sent hotel information that used to go to Anne's house in the two of their full names, and also filled out a few of those postcards that are stuck in magazines with Dave and Anne's name sent to their address. Dave never cared that mail was being sent to Anne at her home from the hotels in which they stayed. It took forever to get the hotels to stop sending that mail. Anne also recommended to Dave's boss that Dave should visit their Employee Assistance Program, as he was in need of counseling in her opinion. When his boss did not reply, she wrote back to him and said forget it, that she was trying to help him lose his job just like Dave had done to her (Dave had given Anne advice as to how to handle her boss when he was so awful. She should not have taken that advice. Women don't stand up for themselves in the South). That was only partially true, as she did believe he needed therapy. His sister, who is a licensed social worker had stated that he was a narcissist, and Anne thought he should be tested for sociopathy due to his inability for empathy, compassion nor had the capacity to truly apologize. In truth, Dave had "mentored" Anne concerning her speaking up to her boss because she had complained about the terrible treatment she had received from her boss. She had started taking an anti-depressant in October, and told her boss that she was doing this to try to cope with her job. The boss treated his employees terribly, and paid no attention to labor laws, even though he himself was an attorney. In January, she was terminated and replaced by a friend of the family. Anne was happy to hear that this relatively young woman was able to walk off the job after about nine months, telling the owner that she was never going to let anyone talk to her like that.

So, after all of the battling of texts and e-mails, Anne asked if she could talk to Dave one more time to clear up all of this mess. Jann finally agreed and Dave e-mailed Anne and asked her to promise it would be the last time she contacted them if he called for closure. Anne answered: "Sounds good."

So, early in May, Dave was "allowed" to call Anne. He asked if she wanted to use Facetime so Anne could trust that he was alone. She told him that she had to cancel all of her social media accounts because of Jann's continued threats, and did not have an iPhone, so had no access to Facetime and did not want to Skype. Jann could always be standing in the hallway where Anne could not see. It was apparent that by this time Anne had lost all of the trust she once had in him.

The phone call was inconclusive. There was no remorse, apology or anything from Dave's end. All Anne was asking for was an apology from all of the threats and bullying she had received during the past several months. She had apologized to everyone for all of the things they thought Anne had done from David and Jann's lies, even though Anne still refused to admit to things they lied about, such as sending them things from Amazon Prime. Anne didn't even have a Prime account and she never sent them anything. Amazon contacted them in August once again and told them they could not bully her about sending things any longer, yet Dave and Jann knew who sent the packages and refused to apologize for those threats to Anne. When asked who sent the packages, they answered that they didn't know, even though Amazon had told Anne differently.

Prior to the final phone call, Anne had received a long text from Jann telling her how God had saved their marriage, but that she wouldn't know anything about that because Anne was an atheist. So, Anne called Dave at work and asked him one thing: "Do you believe in God?" He answered "yes" as if that were a strange question after all of the years he had convinced Anne that he was an atheist as well. Agnostic was never a word he used, but was a blatant atheist. No questions asked. Anne hung up. Yet another lie.

Then Anne received an e-mail saying she had promised to never contact them again after that final phone call. Anne showed them a copy of the e-mail that stated "sounds good," and replied that the word promise was never said by her, and that it was "overused and meaningless," and she never stated that she promised.

Anne wanted so much to tell Tom why she had tried to commit suicide. He did not want to know, although he might have considered an affair to be an option, but loved her so much he did not want to think that could happen. Because Anne and Tom had been having problems over his drug and alcohol abuse, Anne knew that Tom would be upset but would forgive her and understand because he was that type of person. Anne started bleeding internally from the stress. However, Tom may never know about the reason behind the suicide attempt, as he is not a reader of books. And, unless a friend tells him about it, he will prefer to remain oblivious. She told all to her elderly mother, who was never really close to her, and she was interested but noncommittal nor truly concerned. She had no idea how sick Anne really became and was mostly concerned about her own health. Mary was a hypochondriac, but never wanted to go to the doctor because she feels they were out to get her. However, she had to go to the hospital a few times when she broke her wrist when she fell when walking so fast (that doctor gave her medicine that, according to Mary, made her bleed because he was in cahoots with Anne's dad and his lover and they tried to kill her via medicine so she says, and when her hip "collapsed" — she refuses to say her hip broke— or when she bled so badly from a nose bleed and once from diverticulitis). Oh, the story about Anne's dad's lover is most likely a fabrication, but a story that fairy-tale Mary believed to be true. She also believes that William built a room upstairs in the attic over their bedroom for his lover. Let's see, their house had a hip roof, their bedroom was farthest from their entrance to the attic, and that would mean they would have to crawl quite a ways to get to the "room" in which you wouldn't even be able to stand up. A hotel or even a car would have been easier and more enjoyable.

Anne called the police department in Dave's county to see what she would need to do to stop being bullied from them, and to file a suit regarding the threats, including those of physical harm to Tom. They said to bring all documentation to them and they would file a suit. So, in early October, while in severe pain, Anne flew up to his county courthouse with printouts of each email and text she had received with all of the threats. Anne never once threatened them. So, after the young officer glanced through the paperwork of at least 500 sheets of paper, he told her he didn't have enough to file a complaint, even though she had highlighted each and every threat and blackmail item. Anne returned home, feeling abused and depressed.

Towards the end of October, Anne ended up in the emergency room in Charleston. She was on a lot of pain medicine and hallucinating on Dilaudid. She sent an email or text to Dave's work that just said "In hospital." When she was released from the hospital a week later, Anne received a notice from Dave and Jann's attorney telling her not to contact them anymore or they would place a restraining order against Anne. She was especially not to speak with Dave's mother, Donna. Anne had not talked to her since March, when Dave's sister had requested that she not speak to her any longer, even though Donna had sounded as if she wanted to chat. Anne did what had been requested. The request about not contacting his mother was not needed, as that was a non-issue at that time. Anne was sure that Dave's wife had told their attorney that Anne had called his mom, so that part was thrown into the letter, which was immediately shredded upon reading the part about Dave's mom. Anne was still under the influence of Percocet, and didn't care what the rest of the letter said.

She had been hospitalized several times for the internal bleeding and long bouts of uncontrollable diarrhea, which was finally determined to be a serious case of an auto-immune disease in November of that same year. Even though doctors insist that stress irritates the auto-immune system, they don't know what causes it besides possible heredity. Anne believed that she would not have this disease if it weren't for the stress she went through, as she had had a colonoscopy only a few years before and was told that she was perfect inside and wouldn't need another one for at least ten years. After many hospitalizations, now she has no colon and an ileostomy because her insides were so tremendously damaged.

So, Anne had no longer contacted anyone in Dave's family. The mother had recently passed on, and in the past two years Anne was in the hospital many times (several in the ICU due to near death complications of an incurable auto-immune illness that occurred after her suicide attempt in April).

Anne would be lying if she did not say that Dave had a brilliant mind when it comes to his work. He was addicted to it. However, she would also be lying if she did not say that she thought he had psychopathic tendencies: lying about his lies without even realizing this fact (pathological?), making up new lies, bullying and manipulating others with his charm and charisma until he got what he wanted, narcissism (agreed by his social worker sister), his inability to apologize or feel empathy, and so much more. He would even boast about tricking his family over simple things like changing the water filter in their refrigerator. He wouldn't do it, but would change the label. Amazing what the power of suggestion does to others, especially when speaking about someone you should trust. The family thanked Dave for changing the filter because the water tasted so much better! Anne would call him a pathological liar, but she was not a psychiatrist.

Anne tried to commit suicide only twice in her life and only because of his lies, bullying and indifference. She turned to illegal drugs and alcohol after her first attempt via reckless driving, and used prescription drugs and alcohol the second time. She was told that his ex-wife also tried to overdose from the similar treatment she received from him. Anne had seen the scars on Dave's son's arms from when he tried to kill himself over David's actions. She was told by his aunt that it was because he really didn't want his dad to marry Jann, who had accused him of several things he did not do. Anne had seen poor Ben tremble in fear when she had mentioned Jann's name, so she believed that the reason of his suicide attempt was what she had been told. They did not discuss it.

So, why are people like Dave able to live a "normal" life while he destroys the lives of others? When will society stop the abuse and send these bullies and psychopaths to jail or psychiatric hospitals? So many innocent, or gullible, lives have been ruined and those who are responsible are lying their way to innocence, using more untruthful statements and bullying techniques.

When will life justice be served? There is no God, nor Karma nor afterlife in Anne's mind. She feels we need peace and love on earth. Drugs and alcohol would no longer be needed to abolish physically and mentally abused pain-filled lives. If we want to stop drug use in the United States, we must get to the mental pain and suffering that encourages the need to escape reality.

Just look at Anne's, Sally's and Ben's stories of suicide attempts. All three of these people now have that information in their medical files, and are most likely all taking medication for depression and other psychological issues. Yet Dave and Jann are living as if they are untouched even though they were the certain cause for each of these suicide attempts. They are probably both sociopaths, especially since Jann truly believes she is a clairvoyant and was unusually brutal with her threats. They are the ones who should have a record. They have caused others to harm themselves with drugs (prescription and street), alcohol and self-destruction. Our society needs to pay more attention to the bullies that are not only children. Police need to pay attention when people ask for help, and not brush it aside just because a death has not occurred - yet. It is so easy with the Internet and telecommunication sources available to us to do tremendous harm to others.

Bullied by Parents and Spouses

The person who returned this survey has been bullied her entire life. It started out when she was very young, and tried to commit suicide many times. She was abused physically and sexually when young, and was married twice. Both marriages were to men who physically and psychologically abused her.

She then became terrified of her parents, attending a giant new school with a lot more bullies. She had no confidence and no relationships. She felt she married the wrong people just to be married.

Her reasons for suicide attempts included the following: regretting something she had done, abuse physically and mentally by another, lack of self-esteem, feeling of no purpose in life and thoughts of any god or power that did not listen or care for her. She feels that people will often bully others simply because of physical and psychological/mental illnesses. Self-esteem is erased when abused. No one needs someone who is "crazy"! If there is a God, he's a mean fucking son of a bitch. Being ill can harm others.

She feels much of the bullying was done by narcissists. She spoke of a teacher who had a nervous breakdown after a student dropped his class after calling the student a moron. As far as pathological liars are concerned, they won't admit their lies, even when caught, causing trust issues. She groups the lying and narcissism in the same categories.

She has known several people with PTSD, having grown up during the Vietnam War. Not only has she met several GIs with issues, she has also helped many homeless, who will become afraid of a noise or someone getting too close or afraid of change of any kind. Some people seemed to be one person, then later on, another, then back to the first person. She was not sure if this was part of PTSD, or if the others have had DID or were bi-polar. The homeless remain undiagnosed.

Bullied as a Child

Although this was a survey returned via mail, it was from a subject known to us. He replied that he was never physically abused, but was only mentally abused in grade school by bullying, as he was very slender and not very athletic. Although he did not mention this, he was raised by a single mom and her parents from the time he was 6 years old, and was extremely over-protected by all of them. There was a time when he was very small that the only thing he would eat was scrambled eggs, mashed potatoes, flavored gelatin water and potato chips. Once his grandparents took charge by taking him to school and picking him up, they slowly taught him to eat balanced meals, much to his chagrin.

He believes that his father was a narcissist, who cheated on his mother (wife of nine years) and on his second and third wives. In his estimation, this was done because his father enjoyed the confidence boost, as his father was a very gentle and personable soul. Everyone liked his father, whose second wife called up his mom to say she must have been awful to him since he was so nice. He was also good looking, which did not hurt his ego. A few years later, the new wife called his mom to apologize, saying that his dad was now cheating on her, and why didn't she warn her? Even though the dad also cheated on the third wife, she was so wealthy that she held the reins in the family. Either he stayed faithful to her or he would be gone, losing many luxurious benefits he had learned to enjoy. It has been said that after his father suffered a heart attack he became a "faithful" husband.

He felt that most of us have known a pathological liar. We know that his father was, as he always made up a new excuse for not being home while he was out with his different women. Did he think his wife was stupid enough to believe that it took three hours to pick up a pack of cigarettes at the nearest gas station?

He also mentioned a former coworker who would tell them pretty outrageous things about himself regarding wealth, possessions, a supposed spouse, etc. While no one ever confronted this man about these stories directly, probing questions about his stories would sometimes reveal inconsistencies. The stories were always geared towards impressing the co-workers, but most never were.

This gentleman, now in his forties, has become quite confident in his adult life. He had already moved from his home and married a very strong-willed woman. His mother passed after remarrying a widower, and the gentleman moved his family out west away from everyone. He now lives a very happy life in a good climate with two wonderful children and a loving wife.

Mental Abuse —
Anonymous Survey Response

Married twice to men with narcissistic personalities, one suffering from PTSD as well.

This person has had thoughts of suicide due to being mentally abused, being married twice to men that consider themselves important and wanted her to do everything for them without any appreciation. She has attempted suicide, but stopped herself.

This woman feels she has been mentally abused, has a lack of self-esteem and often feels she has no purpose in life. She feels unappreciated for all of the things she does for everyone, and works so hard to please everyone else, including her grown children that she forgets to care for herself.

She feels she is married to a narcissist. Her husband has very low self-esteem, so he constantly will cut people down. He is also a pathological liar, but lies only occasionally. However, he doesn't think it is a bad thing, yet she never knows if he is telling the truth or not, which adds to her feelings of mental abuse.

Showing traits of being a psychopath, her husband blames everyone for any problem. He is NEVER at fault for anything! People need to take responsibility for their own mistakes instead of blaming family and friends. He also has PTSD from Vietnam, and uses it as a crutch for why he can't do things. She has helped her husband through many crisis periods, and loves him very much. They did separate for a few months, only to realize they missed each other and found it to be more difficult to be away from each other.

In school she was made fun of for bucked teeth and being overweight. She was also the last one picked for sports. Her own self-esteem was very low. There was no physical abuse in her case.

Fortunately, she never turned to drugs as her support, although she does enjoy alcohol once in a while to make her feel better and uplift her spirits. Her husband is not supposed to drink due to prescribed medication, yet does upon rare occasion.

Thoughts from a Social Worker

This Licensed Clinical Social Worker specializes in Senior Care.

She has known many narcissists. Most have trouble maintaining relationships and believe they have no responsibilities, never accepting blame for anything.

Her view on pathological liars is that they, too, have difficulty with relationships and are often products of low self-esteem. When it comes to sociopaths, she has worked with patients who have anti-social traits or a serious lack of concern or empathy for anyone.

This social worker has had friends as well as patients with Post Traumatic Shock Disorder as well as Dissociative Identity Disorder. She feels that patients with DID are very discriminated against because others often think of these people as "crazy" rather than ill. Society, in general, lacks the understanding of this illness, which is caused by abuse.

As opposed to many that go into the field of social work, this person does not appear to have any type of emotional or physical abuse imposed on her during her life, but is very sympathetic to those who suffer. Because of her training, she is unable to discuss individual cases and has high ethical standards.

Random Obituaries

The following obituaries were taken from newspapers in the same region of the country. Not wanting to disrupt the lives of the families, their identities have been masked.

Carol xxxx, 19xx-2017

Carol xxxx, xx, of XXXX City passed away Tuesday, xxx. 3, 2017 at her home.

A remembrance gathering of family and friends will be held from 2-4pm on Saturday, xxx. 28, at the XXX Memorial United Methodist Church Fellowship Hall…Visitation was held 6-8pm xxx. 5…

She graduated from XXX XXX High School in XXX, Class of 19xx. Carol graduated from University of XXX, and received a BA in Business and Psychology. She then went on to complete a course of study to earn her license as a local pastor for the United Methodist Church.

Carol married xxx xxx…and made a home in XXX. There they had their daughter on xxx,xxxx. They then moved to XXX to further her husband's career at xxx while Carol worked at XXX Hospital. They then moved to XXX, in xxxx and were blessed with a son in xxxx through adoption. Carol liked to say she had twins at age 7. In xxxx, the family moved to XXX.

Carol made a career at XXX Hospital, in administration, and served as Hospice Chaplain for XXX Health Care and for XXX Hospital in XXX. She then became administrator for XXX XXX Christian Village of XXX.

For the last four years Carol had been battling with mental illness. Her health became a priority and required her to take an absence from her career. Through her time of healing, Carol loved to spend time volunteering. She loved to volunteer at the Humane Society, walking and loving on dogs. She also received joy by providing meals to those in need. She was an amazing cook and loved to care for others. She also spent time with her daughter, XXX, in her 3rd grade classroom. She loved helping kids learn to read.

Mental illness is a serious disease. It effects (sic) even the most loving and motivated people. This disease was not a choice. It effects (sic) the brain and effects (sic) the lives of everyone involved.

Survivors include xxx…

She was preceded in death by her father…

Online condolences may be expressed through xxx

**We must congratulate this family for choosing to mention mental illness. It shows that, although she was suffering, she was still able to carry on a useful existence. We do not know the reason for her death. Mental illness does not mean uselessness.

Although the cause of death was not mentioned for another young woman who died at the age of 32, it was requested that donations be sent to the American Foundation for Suicide Prevention. The obituary included information about her love for animals and her infectious laugh.

A young man, aged 35, died at his home. It was noted that he was giving, caring and a free spirit. Again, cause of death was not listed, but memorial donations were requested to go to the National Institute for Mental Health Gift Fund.

Throughout the country: We found that more people are willing to share their sad loss of family members via their obituaries, and are hoping this brings awareness to the American culture. Browsing an Illinois newspaper on a particular week, two obituaries mentioned suicide, one of a young adult and the other for a gentleman in his mid 40s. A South Carolinian newspaper included an obituary of suicide and another of drug overdose on one particular day.

Mental illness and depression are too common. Drugs are often over or under prescribed, or people who are suffering simply cannot afford to go to a psychiatrist or medical doctor for assistance. If we want to lower the number of suicides or even violence of any type, whether domestic abuse or mass shootings, funds should be available to all American citizens for mental health as a preventative service. We should also be educated in signs of addiction, depression or other mental illnesses. Some people will not even consider the fact that they might need help. If it becomes the norm for all to seek therapy, or to require a mental health exam at an annual physical, then the stigma of meeting with a psychiatrist would no longer be an issue.

The Sergeant's Story
Written November 2017

❦

I met the Sergeant a year and a half ago, but didn't call him that until late last August when a mutual friend died and we started sitting outside together where it was quiet and we could talk. Every loud or unexpected noise made him jump up, sit down, start to shake and leave the area.

I don't know how old he was, but he and his twin brother enlisted in the army at age 17 and served ten years each. They both were in World War II.

Sarge and his twin were farm boys, not very good in school as they missed a lot due to chores. Their parents died within weeks of each other when the boys were 14 years old. The farm and the house went to the bank (probably not rightfully), but they didn't have anyone to help them find the deed, amounts due and paid, etc. They were allowed to sell their animals: eight chickens for $8.00, a rooster for $2.00, two grown pigs ready for market for $6.00, three milking cows and two bulls for $15.00. They lived in a boarding house, sharing a room, one meal a day and one bath per week for $8.00 a week. Then they sold their horses that a grandfather gave them when they were 6 years old. Sarge's brother didn't speak to anyone at all for about 6 months after that. They received $25.00 for the horses, so three more weeks in the boarding house. Both of them did every job, errand and simple work they could find. They missed so much school that they quit and soon joined the army.

Sarge and his brother were very nervous, unworldly men. Their father and mother drank and fought verbally and physically with each other. They were simply threatened the boys. Their dad had a shotgun. If they had a kitten or a dog, the father would get crazy, drunk, and mad, then shoot the animals in front of the twins.

Originally they'd planned to be in the army for 20 years. Sarge's brother never got above Private, First Class. With all of the trauma they already suffered in their childhood, the war was a horrible place to be. Both became alcoholics thanks to the USA government making sure there was booze, beer, cigarettes and drugs to keep them awake as much as possible, a practice that has grown in alarming rates now.

When the twins were discharged from the army they took their bedrolls and clothes and moved under a local bridge. It had been an old train trestle, but now was quiet and unused. Neither of them talked to anyone trying to move to their spot, so this discouraged company and they were left to live on their own. They each received a small military disability pension. They had someone from their past who had their checks mailed to him. Sarge and his brother went and picked up their checks on the third of the month. For $10.00 their "friend" took them to the liquor store and the Hostess day-old store. They bought everything they could for the month. Sarge said they'd eat at a shelter now and then. They drank a lot every day, but what they had lasted all month.

The third winter under the bridge, the twin got a cold and cough that wouldn't go away. They were both afraid of anyone with authority, so going to the doctor was out of the question. Sarge helped him drink and laid on top of all of all of their clothes and on top of his twin. They were both wrapped in his blanket to keep him warm. One morning, his twin didn't wake up.

Sarge remembers running down streets yelling for help. He said he was so crazed that the noise and people didn't bother him. A policeman picked him up and they went to get his twin. Sarge made sure he had a nice funeral and was buried in a Veterans' Cemetery with a bronze plaque. He received the flag from the coffin. The worst part of this story is that the funeral director, the policeman, two veterans that Sarge didn't know and Sarge were the only ones at the service. When he whispered this story to me, he kept giving me tissue and even patted my hand, twice. I just couldn't stop the tears from pouring down my face.

The policeman took Sarge to the V.A. hospital for an evaluation. Because of his age, alcoholism and malnourishment he was sent to a nursing home. At that time there wasn't a home for veterans here or there wasn't a bed for him. He was so traumatized by change that ever moving there was out of the question.

As an aside, I, one of the authors of this book, put myself in a rehabilitation facility because my "pain doctor" had me on way too many pills. I was the only civilian there at the time. That was in 2007. Those poor people had screaming nightmares; all of them had many triggers to set off the PTSD. Some had a type of palsy from excessive drug use, migraines, shock, and were terrified of what they were capable of doing, and horrified and shamed by what they'd done in the Middle East, all of it blocked by pills, dope and booze which was courtesy of the United States Armed Forces. The stories they choked out in group sessions are still part of my nightmares.

Back to Sarge. The twin was injured in a fire fight. It left him with a bad knee and he couldn't walk without a cane and rarely moved from his blankets in the winter. Sarge had hearing loss, but worse than that he shook all of the time, didn't speak loudly enough to be heard if other people were nearby and talking. He'd get upset by a sound, by being spoken to, by being embarrassed from a nurse singling him out for medicine or aides trying to get him to eat at a table. He never did. His tray was set on an end table near the television and he waited until almost everyone was out of the dining room before he quit pacing and sat down to eat. This was the Sarge I knew.

He was also gentle and kind, and grieved deeply when his roommate died. He helped an old woman in or out of the door to the smoking area. He fell last winter. He was already thin, but had lost a noticeable amount of weight. He lost the ability to walk, then to dress himself, and then needed assistance to eat.

I played cards with Sarge's roommate once in a while. Sarge came along to the dining room but sat several feet away. Eventually he would say "hi" to me because I always said "hi" or "how are you doing?" or "What's up, Sarge?"

He finally was able to stay in his chair by the TV when I'd sit in the one next to the end table. At first he bolted away. I told him that he hurt my feelings when he ran off. He told me several times that he was sorry.

Sarge passed away about two or three weeks ago. I hadn't seen him in a long time. When I asked about him, I was told he died two weeks earlier. They do that in nursing homes a lot. We become close; some are like family members, but they aren't honored with a photo or a candle. They're secretly disposed of so no one knows. We all understand that 96% of the people in here leave feet first!

His roommate died unexpectedly and we had small conversations. This story was told to me over the course of five months. I felt very privileged that he told me his story and that I met a human being who was glad for quiet. He began to enjoy not being totally alone. He was proud to be a Veteran and an American. He was a very decent man who had been totally damaged before he was old enough to live a normal life.

Suicide and Overdose

A Sad Heroin Story:

There was an article printed in a small paper some years back regarding a father who was in pain due to his son's suicide by overdose, and the father's attempt to raise awareness about substance abuse. His 20-year-old son died of a heroin overdose.

This was not a story about any "bad" people. The family was middle class, and the son was an average student who often worked for charities distributing food and clothing to the homeless. However, the son became depressed because he did not make good enough grades to attend college. His doctor prescribed drugs such as Xanax and Adderall. The Xanax alone was so expensive that the son found that heroin only cost $5 per day rather than the $30 for Xanax. Because of the cost of the drugs, the son turned to stealing electronics to pay for his habit.

The father now speaks up about drug abuse and recognizing the signs of addiction. Jail only encourages drug use and does not correct the problem. He knows that his son would not want anyone to suffer, and that we need to care for each other.

No one really knows if the son committed suicide or if the overdose was accidental, but the father wants people to understand that there are no stereotypes for addicts.

Suicide Rates Among Farmers:

It is a known fact that the number of individual farmers in the United States is declining rapidly. Many of these farmers are losing property that has been in their families for generations. A farmer knows how important they are to the world by supplying food and nourishment to the population and become depressed when they lose their ability to provide for their families and communities.

What people don't know is that farmers have an extremely high suicide rate. One study from the Centers for Disease Control (CDC) estimated from research that those working in agriculture have a suicide rate of 5 times that of the general population. One of the reasons for this is because of the lack of psychological help. This number could be skewed by possible overdoses from poorly-made illegal substances taken for depression, yet identified as suicide.

Farmers feel isolated, and when they are in despair they have nowhere to turn. The University of Illinois College of Medicine's Department for Rural Health Medicine (RMED) honed in on the need for medical and psychiatric help in the rural communities. Some farms are so remote that there is no medical help for hundreds of miles, and often not available in their own state. There is also a stigma for farmers of the thought of the need for psychological help. Systems were set up so that psychiatric assistance would be available to rural patients via teleconferencing, thus the sessions could be anonymous. Similar programs have been established in other Midwest communities in Wisconsin, Iowa and Kansas.

Federal programs have been discussed, yet not funded. In 1985, farmers gathered in Washington, DC to protest the economic farm crisis. The first Farm Aid concert to raise awareness was also in 1985, and presented in Champaign, Illinois. The RMED program did receive federal funding for rural health in general, including issues regarding higher rates of diabetes, pharmaceutical assistance and asthma, as well as a small portion for the psychiatric assistance included in the general medicine section.

Unbeknownst to many, farmers have access to many chemicals to make illegal drugs. In central Illinois alone many farm communities existed of vacant homes with the roofs blown off from manufacture of crystal methamphetamine. Bunkers were set up in the middle of cornfields for quick and easy access to ammonia and similar chemicals for manufacture of substances to sell in the illegal markets. There were so many that no one could know if they were getting a safe product.

The government believes that by eliminating the importation of drugs from the southern border of the United States, that this will put a damper on the drug situation in the US. As you can see from what is mentioned above, many of the drugs are manufactured right here in America's Heartland. If we are going to reduce the addictions of the users of illegal (and overly-prescribed) drugs, we need to concentrate on the psychological issues behind the use of the substance of choice. People are depressed or have other conditions that need to be addressed. If they are not, then those with issues will find a way to find what they need to make them feel better, even if it means making it themselves. During the Great Depression, the homeless often turned to Sterno, and sniffing glue to eliminate the mental pain. Before that, opium was the drug of choice. One can always produce psilocybin mushrooms for a hallucinogenic experience. And, of course, pure grain alcohol is still being produced in the backwoods, even though a less-potent version of moonshine is now available in the retail markets.

As a side note, Vitamin B-12 has been indicated as a mood enhancer even for those who do not show an abnormal lack of that vitamin in their blood serum tests. We need to start focusing on positive ways to assist those who show signs of depression.

The Gang Member

I was 38 years old when my son was born. From my twenties on, several doctors said I'd never be able to have a baby. But, I didn't ever worry about it. I enjoyed every day of pregnancy.

My son and I were very close until he turned 11 years old, although we did have a serious problem when he was in the 2nd grade when I was misdiagnosed as a schizophrenic. I was given Geodon, trazadone and olanzapine. All those medicines caused me to fall asleep every time I sat down or laid down. A very deep sleep.

My son was angry because I slept all of the time, so one evening he took a thin cord and put it around my neck and ran down the hall, pulling it, but it didn't cause a rift between us. It just woke me up and I got some help for him.

We stayed close. He played little league baseball, loved football and was great at those sports. He had friends, and I spent a lot of time being me again. He would drag his mattress into my room to talk, watch movies and talk some more.

Then, one day he changed. My psychiatrist and friends told me it was normal. He was great to everyone else they told me, and I saw it.

But he hated me. He told me and acted like it. He started getting into trouble at school. He would call the teachers names, didn't do his homework and would act up in any way he could.

There was a year's reprieve when he was 13 and a few months into 14. Then everything got insane. I had no idea, but he was experimenting with drugs and alcohol. I was too mentally ill to pay attention, except when he was angry with me. Then he would call me a fucking bitch and wished that I'd die. He acted as if he was going to hit me and spit (the lowest thing on earth in my opinion) on me and then hit me when he threw a small lamp at me and the base hit my head. Blood started pouring down my face. I put him in anger management. This was his second time in the program. The first time was because of an incident at school. My heart had been broken so many times I wondered if there were any pieces left.

Anger management was a joke, so he found new friends and started behaving, being respectful and talking again. His friends were always polite, too. He joined a baseball team with his best friend whose older brother always provided transportation. Sometimes he would spend a night, weekends or days with them.

I was clueless. He was drinking himself into blackouts, as well as doing drugs. Plus, he wasn't wearing red all of the time because he liked the color. He found a new family, one that paid attention to him all of the time and had his back – a gang. Not a kid, fad sort of gang, but an honest to God gun toting, drug carrying and selling gang that operates coast to coast. One of my friend's sons was in a rival gang. He came to me and told me all about it. He also told me he couldn't keep protecting my son from his gang.

So, I moved my almost 16-year-old son across the country to a horrible little town and didn't tell him until we were leaving. He didn't talk to me on the 26-hour drive, or for the next two weeks. After that we had an apartment of our own. If he did talk it was angry, and would let be know every reason why he hated me. We didn't do anything for his

16th birthday because he didn't want to be around me. I managed to say the wrong thing to him, which would make him angrier. He dared me, taunted me and broke things that meant a lot to me. Then, one day I opened his top drawer and found a bag of weed, a huge bag of pills in all sizes, shapes and colors, and a bag of money.

Because we were in a very small town, I knew I had options. First, I called a city quite a distance from us to find a drug rehabilitation center. Then, I called the local police and got a deal for them to cuff him and drive him all the way to the rehab and to scare the shit out of him. On a visiting day about two or three months in the program, I went to see him and he told me everything about early drugs, drinking, the gang, with information I wish I could forget. He said he was kicked off the high school football team for testing dirty, selling drugs, buying, stealing drugs and going into houses to steal from other people.

He was sweet and sorry and loving. Even after he came home he was wonderful, but only for a while. I sent him to rehab once again about a year and a half later. I begged him to leave home. Then, one day he went to an addict relative's house for Thanksgiving dinner. He didn't call or come home for four months.

On Christmas day I sat in the living room, holding my dog and crying. No tree, no decorations, abandoned by "blood" relatives (very terrible human beings) and my only child. I drank two sodas, fed my dog and pulled out a bottle of vodka and a bottle of valium. Obviously, I woke up. I realized that I overused my medicine, and had watched my son go to pieces. I had him in therapy at two, again at seven, and again at ten. He wouldn't tell them anything and wouldn't take his medication.

We were okay and really, really not for several years. I went forty-two days without knowing where he was. I didn't see him for two years or more. He moved away when we were a week away from being roommates.

For a long while all of the separations and horrendous fighting happened when he was involved with meth, coke and alcohol, usually at the same time and for months and months at a time. The last time he went to rehab the therapist received his blood tests and couldn't believe he'd walked in on his own strength because there were so many types and so much of the drugs in his system.

We've healed, each of us. He smokes weed, but not anything else. I don't mind because it helps my arthritis when he shares. He knows that he needs to be treated for whatever mental illness he carries like a dark demon in his head, but I can't convince him to go. I do listen, encourage and love him.

Last week he got "my" tattoo, a beautiful flower that covers the side of his neck. On his leg is a Mother's Day gift to me, which is the drawing of the last page of *The Giving Tree* by Shel Silverstein. Not only did he remember me reading it to him many times, but he told me that I'd always been his giving tree, giving everything I had. We're okay.

I cried.

The "Evil" Bosses

⚛

Have you ever worked for an employer in the Southern United States? Unless working for a very large corporation, of which there are few, employer/employee relationships are often described as "Plantation Management," and federal laws seem to not apply to them. That being said, one of the authors was "fortunate" enough to work for two of these types of employers after growing up in the North, where unions made certain that employees were treated fairly.

However, she had two "doozies" of managers in the North, as well, but the situations were very different. We will discuss them all here.

The first business owner in the South had grown up in the North, but loved the Southern business strategies. Hire all of the illegals you can if they could show counterfeit identification (a lot of employers didn't even care about the identification and would just pay cash under the table so they wouldn't have to contribute to Social Security, Workers Compensation or Unemployment). Alas, that is more difficult to do now with compliance to e-verify being a large issue, but "day labor" is still allowed in the South. She also loved her "legal" drugs. She had been in an accident some years before, and she was in pain, although it seemed there was nothing she couldn't do. Of course, she had doctors in different states prescribing Oxycontin to her, and she used as many tablets as she could during the course of the day, often falling asleep while speaking to her. Her famous words were that "they sprinkled stupid dust" over the beach. Everyone was stupid except for her. People were paid piece work, and, if they didn't work fast enough to make minimum wage, she would have accounting change the hours on their time sheets. The employers in the South seemed to know the law about salary pay and the minimum salary pay of $455 per week, even if the employee did not qualify as an exempt employee. This would prevent them from paying overtime for the many additional hours they would work. As this author was an HR Specialist with certifications, she questioned the owner about the illegal practices in the company and was terminated. She refused the severance package because she did not want to hold back if she were ever questioned about illegal hiring and employment practices. Looking back, she later realized that it was a blessing to leave that place, even though she had to accept a part-time (eventually full-time) position in retail while the economy was doing poorly. She also found out that, even though she was HR Director for over two years, the longest any prior employee was in that position was four months.

After nearly four years in retail where hours were random and one might need to work 24 hours or more in a row over the holidays, the economy finally picked up a little and she was able to find a professional job once again as Office Manager, a position that included all accounting and HR duties. The owner offered her a small salary, which she agreed to take as long as she had a review in 90 days to be increased substantially. At 90 days, the boss couldn't remember the agreement, but finally resigned himself to increasing the salary. He even refused to comply with the first point on the employee law poster he so proudly posted: Upon hire, employee must be given in writing amount of pay, day of pay and number of hours to be worked. In the South, they often don't like to write things down because they believe in a "gentleman's agreement," or handshake, yet they conveniently forget their word. Anyhow, this man, the founding attorney at his law firm, was one of the cruelest men this author had ever met. On one hand, he was all religious as long as the church he attended had a good choir in which he could sing. He insisted on praying before all employee events. Mind you, he had a history of cheating on his first wife and marrying one of his employees, but we are all human, right? And living in the Bible Belt. His son, who had a history of drug and alcohol abuse, had just gotten out of rehab before this author started working there, which she only found out several months after working there. Around the time she was terminated from her employment there, the son ended up in rehab again and also left the firm for a while. The founding attorney had been told by the employee that she was now taking anti-depressants to help her cope with the stresses of the job, and she wanted him to be aware of that. He let her go three months after that, and replaced her with someone he knew that was under forty. So, not only did he violate disability laws, he also ignored age discrimination. He was aware of that fact, which is why he provided a fairly substantial severance package to make sure that nothing was said. He also wrote the severance package agreement stating that the employer could terminate the severance agreement whenever he wished. This author made him change this. Yes, a severance should provide the employer with some safety, but it is only the employee that is allowed to change their mind within a certain period of time.

The founding attorney treated his employees terribly. He changed his pay agreements on a whim, and would treat men better than women, who were often chastised openly for any little thing, such as not being able to read his handwriting. He would yell mercilessly and expected everyone to drop everything if he needed anything, no matter how small. His son was supposed to eventually take over the firm. However, the son, with all of his problems, was just as bad, if not worse, than the father. He actually would say: "I am your fucking boss. What is your problem? Do what I say!" even though he and his father would blatantly ignore federal employee laws. The state didn't have any laws until they started getting in trouble for so many illegal aliens working in the state. Then they used e-verify for employers who had a certain number of employees.

Both father and son were narcissists with psychopathic and sociopathic tendencies. They would never apologize, and would get rid of anyone who tried to do their job properly if they just didn't like them. After all, it was "employment at will," which was their favorite comeback. Several of their employees attempted suicide because of their treatment from them. The author was pleased to find out that the "friend" who took her place as Office Manager left the job in less than a year, and told the boss that no one was ever going to speak to her that way. Fortunately for the replacement Office Manager, she had a husband with plenty of money, so she didn't put up with the abuse for very long.

Of course, the South is not the only one with bad employers. This author worked for a telecommunications firm that was run by an entire Irish Catholic family who thought nothing of fighting, yelling and drinking during work hours. It was so bad that employees hired via temporary agencies wouldn't even come back to work after their first lunch. This author asked specifically during the interview if the company was a family business, as the last place she had worked was handed over to the son who moved the business to Florida where he lived. She had loved working there. When interviewing for the telecommunications firm, she asked specifically if it was a family-run business because she didn't want the same thing happening to her again. She was told that the owner only had one son, who had absolutely no interest in running the business, even though he did casual labor there during the summers when he was on summer break from college. Upon hire, she was introduced to all of fifty-two employees.

All but six of them were related to the owner Mom and Dad, brothers, sisters, brothers in law, etc. So, after nearly two years of hell, she went to work in the not-for profit industry. Pay was less, but benefits were great with a terrific work/life balance.

Working at the museum was wonderful, even though the fund development person left after her first week and she got to take over those duties until they found someone else nearly two years later. Also, the director left after one month there and an awesome interim director remained for over eighteen months. The actual replacement director was hired under his own terms. He was not to answer to the board of directors for anything and he was to be called the president of the museum rather than director. He took all rights away from the large board of directors. Imagine, he had been a politician out East. Since the number of employees was fairly small due to the use of volunteers, the HR portion of the job was not that large, but the accounting was massive due to discretionary funds, operating funds, capital funds, endowment funds, grant management, etc. The person who was in the job prior to her arrival had not been balancing the checkbook properly, had managed to completely mess up two small state grants for which they were under audit upon this author's arrival to the museum. After three weeks, the state asked if she could straighten out the mess because they couldn't figure it out. Three months later, this author provided the state with an organized spreadsheet of the grants and showed them where the money was spent for each portion of the grant. From that time on, the state gave them her name to show others how to properly manage a grant.

Anyhow, the new president of the museum was definitely a narcissist. I think that might be a requirement for anyone who goes into politics, as one must need that positive reinforcement of winning an election. Pay is much better in other venues, so it must be for the power in most cases. There are probably a few good altruistic souls who actually think that they can help their constituents. When the president started to demand that funds be moved around to make it look like he was bringing in more money than he actually was, this author went to the board of directors to tell them the issue she was having, but was told that there was nothing they could do as they had turned over all of their power to him. It was mutually agreed upon that she could stay and work until she found another job, as it was obvious they would not be able to work together. She would have felt badly, but she was just the last of a string of management that left due to his arrogance and lack of ethics. On the positive side, the president was a schmoozer and was not violent in any manner to the employees. However, he was sneaky and employees could not admire him. After a few years he was asked to resign.

So, here we had a great employee who graduated with honors from college with a degree in Human Resource Management with a minor in Accounting. She believed in ethical behavior at work, even if it cost her a job. Under-appreciated in several situations, it was no wonder that this author tried suicide, using legal prescriptions and massive amounts of alcohol, after her professional frustrations as well as a personal crisis topping it all off. What was the meaning of this life?

Words from a Disabled Veteran

❦

I'm Bi-Polar and have PTSD (100% disabled Veteran) who has never been physically or mentally abused except for time served in Vietnam. I have had three serious suicide attempts in my life. All were post-Vietnam. I took three Quaaludes and a quart of scotch whiskey, drove my Fiat at 130 MPH and crashed into a barn with no harm done, and another huge drug overdose ending in hospitalization. I have mildly regretted some things I have done and have lack of self-esteem from actions in Vietnam and losing friends. Letting family down, I could have and should have been more of a person!

Narcissists and pathological liars entered my life during my years of selling drugs, including me to a point when I became a drug dealer, but I now know where to draw the line. With my PTSD, my first time in the hospital I met a murderer who was seriously sociopathic and a psychopath. He threatened patients. I informed him to stop or answer to me. I protect the weak as part of my training. I don't know what that makes me, but I stopped the guy, and scared him.

My Veterans Mental Health doctors have been great. I was in Vietnam from 1969 to 1970. I was diagnosed with PTSD in 1998 and received my benefits in 2001 or 2002. One doctor in 2001 asked me to write three pages describing how I felt at my bottom and lowest point.

Today, I'm pretty solid. I weigh 225 pounds. I still have occasional night terrors and likely always will. But my relationships across the board are good. I have 100% Disability for PTSD from VA and Social Security, so finances are secure, but minimal. PTSD sucks, but it is livable!

As I understand it, PTSD (Post-Traumatic Stress Disorder) has symptoms that occur in three distinct categories: Intrusion, Avoidance and Hyperarousal.

Intrusion:

I have, at times, flashbacks to my time in Vietnam. I wasn't an Infantry-man; rather, I was an Information Specialist with the 32nd Public Information Department of the Headquarters Company of the First Brigade of the 101st Airborne Division. My time was spent almost equally in Basecamps finalizing pictures and stories, on Firebases doing "personal stories and photo ops," and in the field with various units from psy ops (psychological operations), to LRRPs (Long-Range Reconnaissance Patrol), to regular infantry. To be sure, there were the occasional mortar attacks on Phu Bai and even a couple of sapper (reconstruction and re-pairs) efforts, however, for the most part, life in the basecamp was se-cure with a chance for unwinding and doing the mundane of the job.

Firebases were a bit more frightening. Attacks came a bit more often than at the basecamp. I recall my first "search and destroy" mis-sion with a unit of the 2nd of the 327th Infantry off of Fire Support Base Tomahawk. I was scared to death! Nothing really happened. We chased a group of Vietnamese to secure their papers and ensure that they be-longed in the area they were in at the time. The chase through bamboo thickets, tall grass, and down the hills were quick, exhilarating and more than I signed on for. I have flashbacks to this chase on a fairly regular basis. No, it isn't as dramatic as the over-running of Fire Support Base Ripcord where our guys were being dispatched with great regularity.

At Ripcord, I was more an infantryman than a journalist. I had my spot in the bunker, my field of fire and my need to cover my men on each side. I've never had such a fright in my life! I relive Ripcord painfully and altogether too often!

Even one psy ops mission fills my memories and dreams. We went to a village to show films of "Vietnamification" which I thought very ironic. It had to get dark to show the eight-millimeter movie. There were out in a secluded village surrounded by Vietnamese with the darkness enveloping us and the generator pounding in the background. My mind went through all the possibilities, none of which were positive. Nothing happened that night; but in my dreams that is not the case. My dreams were filled with gore and death.

I've become hyper-emotional. f I see an American Flag, an ROTC unit or hear the Star Spangled Banner, I tear up and can hardly control my emotions. I remember the sights, smells, and conditions of my time in Nam. I no longer attend ballgames because I'm seeing in my mind what happened so many years ago. My senses seem to provide real triggers for these flashbacks and nightmares. I can see bamboo thickets near my home, blood in one of those "real-life" films, or even smell certain foods, and BANG—I'll have wicked dreams that night. The sight, or even worse, the sound of a helicopter takes me immediately back to Vietnam. I've almost wrecked the car because I wasn't on the road. I was thinking of how to take cover and protect.

Avoidance:

I internalize emotions for the most part; at times, I break down into tears but I tend to be numb or unwilling to show too much joy or affection. My relationships with my wife and son are strained and the guilt I feel is incredible. My in-laws see this too, and their heart goes out to me and to my family.

I seem to go from absolutely no feelings or emotions to wide sweeping anger and rage. I often wonder if my Bi-Polar Condition came from the PTSD. I never recall experiencing these manic-depressive moods prior to my service in Nam.

When it comes to getting things done, I can no longer work. The emotional problems are just a part of it. I could no longer do the complex work of being a good educator/professor, nor could I complete my doctoral studies. I had to avoid people and situations in order to dodge becoming too emotional or stricken with a panic attack.

I seldom go anywhere. My wife and I used to go places and do things together. Now, I stay at home while she goes and does things. I do try to go to my son's sporting activities, but I focus strongly on what he is doing and not the things around me. I just don't want to be around others unless it is totally on my terms. I now stay at home most of the time.

I can't drive over about thirty minutes without losing concentration and becoming a risk on the road. While at home, I read my mysteries, watch TV and I listen to sports talk radio while I fiddle on the computer. I even do dishes, wash clothes and work on dinner some. KISS: Keep it Simple Stupid! But I am a failure when it comes to providing for my family. Emotional or financial support is beyond my means.

Hyperarousal:

I am beyond paranoid most of the time. I sit in our family room in such a manner that I can see anyone coming from anywhere within the house. The front and back doors are under my control, and no car can approach the drive without my hearing. I have become so irrationally angry at people to be even on the brink of violence. On more than one occasion, I have threatened people who cross me or put me at some level of risk. My memory and ability to concentrate are shot. I used to be outstanding in my mental abilities; now, I am, on my best days, average. This disturbs me in that I can't be what I've always been.

My basic sleep pattern is a mess. Most nights I try to get down between midnight and three in the morning, but, on other occasions I'm so zoned out to the world that I go into bed around eight and just veg out until sleep takes me over. I sleep in the recliner in the family room or in my son's room if he is gone. I haven't shared my wife's bed for some time. My wife has complained nicely that I'm anxious and jumpy a good deal of the time. Small things startle me: noises, horns, barely-noticeable images from my side vision all get me on alert. My life over the past years has become nothing but a series of dealing with misery, despair, guilt and depression. I've often thought of checking out, but that would destroy my wife, and I am frightened at what it could do to my son.

Errata:

In the past few years I've become a mental and emotional shell of what I once was. Physically I've become a mess. I have always been a big man, 225 to 236 pounds, but since having been on so many various medications, I have ballooned to over 350 pounds. That weight and what it constrains me from doing destroys any possibility of any positive mental image of myself. All of the VA doctors offer is another trip to the dietician, who is an idiot. Why doesn't the VA have a bariatric program to help those of us who suffer from being overweight and all of the mental and physical pain it can cause us?

I'm not only emotionally separated from my wife, but physically as well. Last time we were intimate, over 30 months ago, I felt like I was going to die. My heart rate and breathing were terribly accelerated, and I had sharp chest pains. Not only do I feel I have diminished emotional capacity, but my physical situation has injured my feeling of intimacy and normal activity. Hell, I can't walk more than a quarter of a mile or do a half of a flight of stairs without feeling pain in my knees and lower back. If I really push and do any work in the yard or go out and exert myself, I feel I'm near a stroke or heart attack. I'm a prisoner to my emotions, to my past, and to my own physical being.

Add all this errata to the fact that I'm convinced that the Veteran's Office is going to deny my claim for 100% disability, I only feel more the failure. I can't work! The idea terrifies me! If I don't have the disability to support my Social Security, then I don't feel that I'm offering anything at all to the betterment of my household and our lives together. At the very minimum, I need to feel that I provide for them as well as can be hoped. More than once I've prayed to just "throw off this mortal coil" and, after a proper period of grieving, life would be better for all around me; it's just that I don't really believe that. I just feel it at times. To quote from the table of Alcoholics Anonymous, "I'm sick and tired of being sick and tired." HELP!

The Dealer's Account

Mine was not really the typical family, as my mother had three strokes on the day I was born. That experience left her paralyzed on her right side for the rest of her life. It changed our family dynamic completely in that my father changed his job because his insurance was dropped and income could not pay for my mom's bills, let alone pay for household expenses. Dad became a traveling salesman for a large international corporation. We lived in Texas and his territory was Texas, Oklahoma, Louisiana and Arkansas. I was taught how to deal with mom's fairly regular seizures, protect her, and call the ambulance or local friends. I grew up rapidly. All was pretty good until the early summer of 1963 when I was just 13. My father, at the age of 56, died of a coronary. He really was the center of my world, my hero and friend.

My mother's family lived in the Midwest and it only made sense for us to move from my home of Texas to the frozen unknown country of Illinois. I wasn't happy. I was frankly morose, but knew I had to be there for mom. Now, we were poor. Mom didn't want to move in with her mother because she was proud and wanted to be on her own. We couldn't afford it, but we tried for a year. I went to the local Junior High and was NOT popular! I was large for 13 (six foot and 185 pounds). I also spoke with a Texas drawl, which caused participation in several fights. I was miserable. I discovered a few guys and girls who had begun to drink beer. They drank a couple beers and got silly, but I drank six beers and became comfortable. I liked that: comfortable for the first time in six months! High school began and I played football and fell into a faster crowd. On the weekends there were parties with more beer, hard liquor and something new: marijuana! I found a way to cover up my anger at being where I didn't want to be, at feeling awful all the time, and fighting when I knew fighting was stupid even though I never lost a fight. Then I quit football! I met some guys who were really laid back and friendly. They treated me nicely and were kind enough to include me in their activities. They listened to the music I enjoyed and invited me to parties they held. I found a new home. On the up side: more beer, drinking and drugs! No complaints on my side of things.

Over time I began working and going on to college. I just didn't see the point in working forty hours a week and attending college simultaneously. I joined the Army and went off to Vietnam for a year and then to Germany for eighteen months. I thought my friends would disappear, but they kept in touch with letters and tapes the whole time. They helped keep me sane. While overseas there were more drugs and booze whenever possible without messing up my mission. I was really a fine soldier. When I returned home I attended college. I also kept getting more into drinking to cover up the fact that I wasn't happy with where I was at.

While in graduate school for speech communications, one night I was in the bar with my roommate, when my thesis director came in. I was stoned and really loaded. He had to yell in my ear over the bar noise to tell me he had received the news that my mother had died unexpectedly. I yelled back that I had to get home. I was in no condition to drive 350 miles, but my director offered to drive me and dropped me off and turned around and drove back. I was broken again. My mom was only one year older than my father when he died (he was 14 years older than she). I didn't think I'd survive! I was alone in terms of family except for my grandmother and a half-dozen cousins. I finished my Masters and obtained a position teaching at a community college, which was my dream. I was also coaching great speech teams that won national tournaments!

In a period of about fifteen years I went from being a pretty hard drinker and casual drug user to being a full-fledged alcoholic and drug addict. Not even my closest friends had any idea of the amount I was using daily because I was no longer living near them. At that time I had no idea the depths to which I had sunk after a divorce, living on the streets for a bit (even while teaching and being elected by students as the "Best Faculty on Campus")!

I progressed from user to dealer. While in Chicago at a fancy party I met a man of great wealth who became a good friend. We'd travel together at his expense because he liked me. We went to Costa Rica, New York and more whenever I was on break. He offered me a chance to earn some money: dealing drugs! I was really good at it, a natural born salesman. He told me I just couldn't tell anyone I knew because they were liabilities, only new clients or clients that my friends might have, but in small quantities. But if I talked, I was dead! At one time I was selling between $5,000 and $7,000 per week of cocaine. This went on for about a year. I paid off all of my debts, bought two different cars, one of which was brand new, and traveled more than I could have ever afforded while in grad school. Then, my friend was killed and I disappeared. I removed myself from all of my connections and common friends. I drank a lot. I was terrified, afraid the police would come or even more afraid "others" would come. I tried three times to commit suicide and failed. God, or conditions, intervened.

On November 16, 1982, I quit drinking and drugging after a period of over 20 years. I have had a few times where with a couple of old friends, I lifted a few beers in celebration, but now my life is largely clean and sober. I am a Christian and try to live that life faithfully. I try to accept people and situations for what they are, but I have my values: God, Family and Country.

ELDER ABUSE

Elder Abuse is such a huge topic and can turn in so many ways, from abandonment, to physical abuse, or severe mental abuse. The elderly have lived through many types of events, and love to share their stories.

We all have family arguments, but sometimes they escalate into traumatic mental events. These disagreements will eventually turn into a mutual consensus that everyone was a little at fault and that bygones will be bygones and start anew.

Other times, the arguments become so out of control that they can never be repaired. Children will dump their parents off at nursing homes, never to be seen again. Or, they continue to be so hateful that the parent has to separate themselves in order to avoid abuse. That is an extremely difficult thing to do for most parents.

Take, for example, one woman who told her daughter of an intimate troubling detail of her life and the suicide attempt that ensued from the bullying she received after the qualifying event, thinking that the daughter would accept her honesty, as the daughter was always receptive to her own friends who were in trouble of one type or another. The mother had endured her daughter's shoplifting arrest, multiple auto accidents, sexually transmitted diseases and therapy. This particular discussion took place at breakfast the morning before the daughter's engagement party. The mother had flown in from many miles away to attend this event. The father would not fly, and there was not enough time available for either of them to take time off of work long enough to drive for this occasion. Trains take even longer than a drive, so that was not an option.

The mother had thought that she and her daughter were very close due to the many obstacles they had overcome, and that is the reason she confided in her daughter. She thought her daughter, in her 30s, would certainly accept her mother's one transgression in her adult life. After all, everyone is human, and we all have our faults, daughter definitely included.

Anyhow, the mother was completely ignored by her daughter and son at the engagement party, but, fortunately, mom knew enough people to make the time endurable. She had accompanied the daughter and fiancé to the party, so had no vehicle to escape.

After a few days when the mother had returned home, the daughter made it known that the mother had totally ruined her engagement party for her because of their morning discussion. The mother apologized and commented that she had no idea that the conversation would have that type of effect on the daughter, or else she wouldn't have discussed it at that time. Of course, mom couldn't believe the response she received, so she explained that none of her friends had ever heard of an engagement party, and that must be something rich bitches do up north. That comment, of course, was meant to be a jab, even though those words actually had been said by the mother's old officemates. Mom was out of work and could not find any jobs due to the poor economy, her age (in her 60s), and the beginning of an incurable illness which created a secondary reason for the suicide attempt. She had been on a strong anti-depression medication for quite some time, but it wasn't working, so the daughter's tantrum brought out the worst in her.

After the mom's suicide attempt of massive quantities of prescription opiates, valium and nearly a bottle of Belvedere vodka, she started having internal bleeding, and was having this issue during the engagement party trip. Of course, this was the future bride's event, so she wasn't thinking about the mother's physical pain, even though the daughter knew that mom was constantly in the bathroom. The mother confided in her daughter at breakfast to let her understand why she was not her usual self due to the pain and the complication of blood that was constantly oozing out of her rectum.

The argument did not end. The daughter explained that she needed her space and would not be able to talk to her mother for a while. So mom did not contact her for a month when she sent an email of a recipe like they used to do in the past. The mother was instantly informed that she obviously didn't know what "space" meant. Then, about another two months went by with no communication, and mom sent another recipe or a joke to test the waters. Again, mom was told she didn't understand what "needing her space" meant. At that time, mom was on Percocet for her pain, so was a little more relaxed with her tongue. She questioned the fiancé to see if he really wanted to marry this woman who was treating her mother so badly over a rather small thing.

Of course, the daughter, who was never really close to her brother, became best buddies with him. They started meeting for lunch because they worked fairly close to each other even though they lived over an hour from each other. One day, when the two went out to lunch to complain about mom, the daughter read the texts from the mom to the son stating that the daughter was being a bitch to her, and was there anything he could do to help.

In the meantime, the mother ended up in the hospital in October with colon, intestines and rectum so inflamed that the hospital could not read the CAT scan nor perform a colonoscopy. She remained in the hospital for a week to try to control the constant diarrhea and bleeding. They put her on such strong pain medicines that she hallucinated and fell out of bed. While under the influence of Dilauded, she texted the children to tell them she was in the hospital and the father did as well, letting them know how seriously ill mom was. The only response from the daughter was that she tried to send mom flowers but the gift shop was closed. That's the best she received during a full week in the hospital. Like there are no other florists in the large town of Charleston? Mom didn't even care about the flowers, but some sort of get well acknowledgement would have been appreciated. A kind word is all the mother would have wanted. She didn't need the abandonment of her children. She needed and wanted them.

In November, after tons of medicines including multiple steroids, the inflammation had gone down enough for a colonoscopy and endoscopy to be completed. It was determined that the mother had Sudden Onset Severe Crohn's Disease. Now, the specialists can't tell you why Crohn's happens, but there are strong indications that it is hereditary and becoming much more common. Since the mother had been given a clean bill of health from her colonoscopy only a few years prior to this event, she would tell anyone that the disease is caused from stress. Even experts do admit that stress exacerbates the symptoms and should be avoided at all costs.

Her children would not talk to her, but the mom tried to speak to them on occasion. One morning in January, the son called mom up at 7 am in the morning to yell at her for being such an awful person. This was a one-sided scream fest that lasted close to an hour. Mom said nothing. She let him vent. When he was done and had hung up, she took out two boxes and sent personal memorabilia with a passionate letter to each child saying that she was in extreme pain, the doctors had told her to avoid all stress, and that she had no alternative but to disown the children after a long, unfortunate period of anger. She could no longer take the abuse and it was necessary for her health to avoid all contact with them if they could not be civil. Addresses were erased from her phone for text and calls, and all email addresses were blocked. She didn't want to catch herself calling them up in a moment of love only to be chastised for being so evil. A few months after she sent the packages to her children, she sent her son the information from the Crohn's Association and told him there was a good indication that it was genetic. Of course, he sent an email stating that he received the "poor me" information. She told him it was only sent for his benefit, as he had complained of intestinal problems in the past. If she wanted to say "poor me" it would have included the many additional complications she had endured.

It must be mentioned here that not only had the son been arrested for spousal abuse in the past while he was under the influence of alcohol, but he always pushed the rules to the limit. That is probably why he is a stressed-out but successful executive in a global firm. His wife worked part time and took classes to learn new-age techniques in healing, such as Reiki. It most likely cost more for her classes than the income she brought in, forcing the son to put more stress on himself to succeed. He also bought a huge house with a swimming pool. His parents could never afford anything like that, so one can only assume that he wanted to prove he was a success or that his wife wanted a substantial step up. Either way, the son, in his 30s, has many serious stress-related health issues. His mom was concerned about him.

Although parents do not expect loyalty from their children for all of the work they put in raising them, they also don't expect disrespect. The children's parents were blue-collar workers, but made sure their children had the best education (Montessori, gifted, creative and performing arts, etc.) and made certain the children were allowed and encouraged to participate in any activity they desired (dance, theatre, figure skating, poms, miscellaneous sports as well as volunteer events). The parents were encouraging college, but let the children know that they could not afford to provide anything but books, fees, and a small monthly stipend. Either one of the children had a good chance to earn full-paid scholarships. The son had an IQ that they stopped counting at 179 because after that it was irrelevant. Unfortunately, school did not interest him, and he preferred to skip school. Every day the mother would come home from work to get a message that he had missed some or all of his classes. Discussions did not help. He barely passed his classes due to poor attendance. He did receive a small theatre scholarship from the local entertainment league who informed him that they really didn't want to give him the award because he was arrogant, but he was very talented and had even opened his own not-for-profit children's' theatre when he was 16, begging his mother to incorporate for him because a corporation needed to be formed by someone 21 years of age or older. She complied. She loved her children and would do anything in her power to help them pursue their dreams.

So nearly a year goes by with no contact, even though the children were furious that they had been disowned due to their improperly-timed cruelty to their mother. They never attempted to reconcile. It was killing the mother.

In August, though still ill, the mother and father (much against his wishes) flew up to the north to spend time with her mother, who was 85, and to drive her car home, as there was no reason for her to keep the car after her hip surgery and no valid driver's license. They did not tell the children, who lived less than two hours away, because they wanted it to be an enjoyable trip with no confrontations. The son, who had kept in contact upon occasion with his father, found out that mom and dad were on vacation. The son finally got the father to explain that they were up north to visit grandma. As soon as that message was relayed, the son contacted the sister to let them know the parents were only a few hours away. While they were packing up to leave, the daughter and her fiancé were sitting in their car across the street from their grandmother's house. When the dad walked outside, the daughter approached the dad and wanted him to sign a form that he had already refused to sign via the mail. She had wanted to be married in the Baha'i faith because her best friend's father was a minister, and had also married her brother. In order to be married in that faith, the parents must sign a "contract" saying that the child had done everything they could to create a happy family. Her dad did not agree with that statement, so he would not sign. He offered to speak with the minister, as the parents knew him quite well. She stormed away saying now she knew how HE felt about her and that he had taken sides with her mom and she never wanted to hear from him again. And he hasn't, although it kills him. He sent her a happy birthday, but received no reply.

In severe pain during the year, with Humira shots being double-dosed still with no effect, in December it was discovered from yet another CAT scan that there was an abscess in the colon and to get to the hospital immediately. Red blood count was down and white blood count was extremely elevated and it was determined that the mother also tested positive for MRSA. Humira was discontinued, and mom was on intravenous antibiotics and steroids. It was just before Christmas, and, although white blood cell count was still quite elevated, all of the doctors were taking off for the holidays. She was given the choice of staying on IVs or going home with multiple prescriptions, only to return in January to have her colon removed. Of course, the mother chose to go home with her significant other for the holidays. That is correct, significant other. The children's father had refused to marry the mother because he did not believe in it. All of his friends had gone through terrible divorces, and his folks did not seem to have a pleasant marriage. Great guy, though. That probably happens a lot, but most couples pretend they are married rather than face the embarrassment of living in sin and having bastard children. They, on the other hand, are proud to admit they've been together well over forty years without any legal ties.

On the tenth of January the mother's colon was removed with great recovery time. Not only did they remove the colon and replace it with an ileostomy, the severe pain was gone and she was discharged only three days after surgery. The nurses were so impressed. She was then required to go to the cancer center to receive iron infusions every few months to get her blood count up.

Although that went well, in February mom ended up in intensive care, only defying death by the use of a special new machine the hospital had acquired. Blood pressure was nearly zero and kidneys had failed due to dehydration. The father let the children know she was in the hospital personally, and also posted on Facebook, but mom never received a phone call or a card or a text.

Finally, on her birthday, the mother received a text from her son, although she had to ask who was wishing her a happy birthday. If you remember, mom had deleted all of their contact information. The response was that it was from her wayward son wishing a happy day. Mom's response was that she would always love him and that he had no idea what that text meant to her. She then felt comfortable enough to text him a happy Thanksgiving, to receive a pleasant reply that it was a good day to be alive. So then she sent him info about an audition for America's Got Talent that was going to be held near his home. No reply about that, but she really wasn't expecting one. He'd always had a soft spot in his heart for the theater. In fact, he met his wife during a production in which they were both participating.

The son was planning to visit his grandmother two days before Christmas with his family. The grandmother, who was called at least once daily by his mother, told his mom this as well as the fact that the daughter and her now husband (no, the parents were NOT invited to her earth-day wedding), were either bringing her lunch or taking her out to eat. So, a few days before the visit, the mom suggested that a great Christmas present for their grandmother would be the washing and changing of her sheets that hadn't been done since his mom had been there in August, and possibly a few bags of water softener salt. Obviously, an 87-year-old woman who can't go up and down the basement stairs is unable to fill her water softener. Well, the son texted his dad and said that mom commanded that he do those things. So mom texted back that it was only a suggestion and not a command, and she felt sorry for him if he felt that way about her. Then he went into a big rant how the mom always tried to make him feel guilty, and so on. He reworded what was said to make him look like the good guy. For example, her text said: "I'm not trying to make you feel guilty. That is your take. So be it."

His response was: "Again. That last message you said: 'It's not my fault, it's yours' You could have ended with 'I'm not trying to make you feel guilty.' Instead, you HAD to get your jab…always. Fuck Off. Merry Christmas." The mother had meant that he had taken it the wrong way. He misunderstood. Text is such an awful way to communicate, but it seems to be the preferred method these days. The mother contacted his wife to say that she was concerned about her son, and the wife replied that the mother had no idea how horrible she had been and that she didn't have any compassion for her children. The wife had never been privy to the nasty phone calls her husband had shared with his mother. Text is probably why the country is so divisive. Take President Trump and his short and ignorant ranting Tweets, for example. He might be a great guy, but certainly does not present himself in that manner.

Anyhow, mom is now on disability and waiting for her first payment. She has been out of work due to physical and mental illness for three years. She has used up most of her retirement funds, and the father used up most of his seven years prior due to surgeries and follow-up treatments for bladder and prostate cancer.

Although most of the physical pain is gone, mom still has many complications from the Crohn's Disease: fistulas and more surgeries, problems with many foods, raw skin by her stoma, shaking hands, and leaking from the ostomy at any time, sometimes on a daily basis. The doctors don't seem to care much anymore now that the colon has been removed, but the problems are aggravating and often painful for sometimes lengthy periods of time. It certainly would be nice to have support from her children, but she no longer foresees that ever happening. She often thinks of suicide once again, and feels like she is wasting space on this planet. As a pacifist, she is not into blood or guns. We hope she stays away from the alcohol and the drugs.

In the meantime, 1300 miles away from her own aged mother, the mom is trying to help her out from a distance, which is difficult since the grandmother is very hard of hearing and has no outside stimulation. She rejects living in an assisted living facility and wants to die in her home, even though there is no one there to help her except for the once-a-week visit from an aide who does her shopping and laundry. The mom does try to get up to see her elderly mother at least one time per year, if not twice, even while being ill herself. The grandchildren (mom's ex-children) only live an hour and one-half away, but only see her on rare occasions.

EPILOGUE

As you can see from the stories included in this writing, many stories of abuse or trauma unfortunately end up in opiate, drug and/or alcohol abuse. It is time for the world to take notice of the fact that it is the mental disorder or poor environment rather than the simple decision to use and abuse addictive substances, including coffee!

Allegedly, one of the founders of the musical group "Pink Floyd," Syd Barrett, was a schizophrenic whose demons were enhanced by the use of opiates and other miscellaneous drugs. It was his mental illness that inspired the famous song "Wish You Were Here" in 1975. Barrett died in 2006 from diabetes complications that arose from his opiate abuse.

In 1995, British service "The Samaritans" used R.E.M.'s song "Everybody Hurts" in their advertising campaign regarding the high suicide rate but low crisis service in the UK.

With so much communication done via the Internet, including Twitter and Facebook, rather than face-to-face interaction, it becomes easier for people to bully others simply because they don't need to look others in the eye. Also, body image is still a huge issue. If anyone does not have perfect hair, or skin or body mass, etc., one can easily become an outcast. All one needs to do is turn on the television for an hour only to be bombarded with one diet or exercise commercial after another.

So, when looking at causes of opioid and other substance abuse, it has come to our attention that it is equally the abuser's fault for this horrible worldwide epidemic. Not only do those with mental disorders, including depression, PTSD, DID and anxiety, have issues, but the abusers, the bullies, the narcissists, the pathological liars, the sociopaths need to be monitored as well. A mandatory mental wellness class should be included at every grade level, with equal importance as physical education, English, Science and Mathematics. It seems like respect to others is often overlooked in these fast-paced days of being tethered to cell phones or tablets to be available for work 24/7. True relationships are hard to find.

Certain types of personalities are helpful in some instances. Narcissists, for example, do well in sales, advertising, acting and politics. And a few fibs now and then must be used to boast a product or service, but that is not the same as pathological lying. Pathological liars continue to lie over their own lies and will lie even more with no regret or admission that they ever said the prior lie. They simply do not remember their prior lies because it is an illness. Sociopaths have no feelings of empathy and will never apologize for anything, even though they are often very hurtful. There is no feeling of compassion. One must feel badly about those who are the cause of trauma as well, and they also require psychological help.

We are hoping these stories will allow others to see themselves or others among the words. It is our hope that people start to speak openly about mental issues as they are now coming forth about sexual abuse. Mental illness is just that, a disease, and people should not be afraid to go to a therapist or physician for assistance. Those with any of the problems listed, and those that were not discussed here, should be elated that we have evolved into a society that recognizes their illnesses, and be thankful that not everyone is placed in an asylum for electric shock therapy or a lobotomy, or even locked in a basement or attic or sent out for an exorcism. Unfortunately, some of those "cures" are still being practiced today.

The pursuit of happiness is included in our Declaration of Independence in the United States. Let's make it available to all.